Educating Media Literacy

Critical Media Literacies Series

Series Editor

William M. Reynolds (*Georgia Southern University, USA*)

Editorial Board

Peter Appelbaum (*Arcadia University, USA*)
Jennifer Beech (*University of Tennessee – Chattanooga, USA*)
Eleanor Blair (*Western Carolina University, USA*)
Ana Cruz (*St. Louis Community College, USA*)
Venus Evans-Winters (*Illinois State University, USA*)
Julie C. Garlen (*Georgia Southern University, USA*)
Nicholas Hartlep (*Berea College, USA*)
Mark Helmsing (*George Mason University, USA*)
Sherick Hughes (*University of North Carolina – Chapel Hill, USA*)
Danielle Ligocki (*Oakland University, USA*)
John Lupinacci (*Washington State University, USA*)
Peter McLaren (*Chapman University, USA*)
Yolanda Medina (*Borough of Manhattan Community College/CUNY, USA*)
Brad Porfilio (*Seattle University, USA*)
Jennifer Sandlin (*Arizona State University, USA*)
Julie Webber (*Illinois State University, USA*)
Handel Kashope Wright (*The University of British Columbia, Canada*)
William Yousman (*Sacred Heart University, USA*)

VOLUME 3

The titles published in this series are listed at *brill.com/cmls*

Educating Media Literacy

The Need for Critical Media Literacy in Teacher Education

By

Allison T. Butler

BRILL SENSE

LEIDEN | BOSTON

Cover illustration: Photograph by Allison T. Butler

All chapters in this book have undergone peer review.

The Library of Congress Cataloging-in-Publication Data is available online at http://catalog.loc.gov

Typeface for the Latin, Greek, and Cyrillic scripts: "Brill". See and download: brill.com/brill-typeface.

ISSN 2666-4097
ISBN 978-90-04-41675-8 (paperback)
ISBN 978-90-04-39615-9 (hardback)
ISBN 978-90-04-41676-5 (e-book)

Copyright 2020 by Koninklijke Brill NV, Leiden, The Netherlands.
Koninklijke Brill NV incorporates the imprints Brill, Brill Hes & De Graaf, Brill Nijhoff, Brill Rodopi, Brill Sense, Hotei Publishing, mentis Verlag, Verlag Ferdinand Schöningh and Wilhelm Fink Verlag.
All rights reserved. No part of this publication may be reproduced, translated, stored in a retrieval system, or transmitted in any form or by any means, electronic, mechanical, photocopying, recording or otherwise, without prior written permission from the publisher.
Authorization to photocopy items for internal or personal use is granted by Koninklijke Brill NV provided that the appropriate fees are paid directly to The Copyright Clearance Center, 222 Rosewood Drive, Suite 910, Danvers, MA 01923, USA. Fees are subject to change.

This book is printed on acid-free paper and produced in a sustainable manner.

In memory of

Jack
May 20, 1927–December 9, 2017
&
Clark
May 9, 1945–October 15, 2018

Husbands, fathers (in-law), grandfathers, and humans extraordinaire

∴

Contents

Acknowledgements IX

1 Education Is the Answer (What Is the Question?) 1
   1   Introduction 1
   2   Main Argument 3
   3   Media Literacy: Foundations 6
   4   Focus of the Book 11
   5   Conclusion 13

2 Critical Media Literacy 17
   1   Introduction 17
   2   How Media Literate Are Young People? 19
   3   Defensiveness to Democratization/Protection to Celebration 20
   4   Critical Media Literacy 23
   5   Technology in the Classroom 26
   6   Conclusion: What's Missing? 29

3 The Education of Training Teachers 30
   1   Introduction 30
   2   History of Teacher Education 31
   3   Teacher Education Debate 35
   4   Arguing with Alternative Teacher Education 37
   5   Arguing with Traditional Teacher Education 43
   6   Commonalities between Approaches 45
   7   Conclusion 49

4 Politicizing the Classroom 50
   1   Introduction 50
   2   Education as Solution 51
   3   Location of Reform 55
   4   Role of the Teacher 60
   5   Role of the Student 66
   6   Classroom Today 68
   7   Conclusion 70

5 Practices of Media Literacy in the Classroom 71
   1   Introduction 71
   2   The Need for Teacher Education 72

VIII CONTENTS

3 Classroom Dynamics 76
4 Subject Relevance 80
5 Connecting Teachers 82
6 Justification for Practice 82
7 Conclusion 84

6 Conclusion: (Media) Education *Is* the Answer 85

1 Introduction 85
2 Many Calls to Action 86
3 Teacher Education in Critical Media Literacy 88
4 Does Media Literacy Work? 89
5 What Is 'Good' Media Literacy? 92
6 How to Do It? 94
7 The Manifesto's Journey 96
8 Conclusion 97

References 101
Index 118

Acknowledgements

The easiest way to write these acknowledgements would be to simply state that without the following people and places, I would be a lost soul. They deserve more words than that.

Thank you to my academic home, the Department of Communication at the University of Massachusetts Amherst. Much of this work was made possible through generous funding from the SBS Dean's Office and the Teaching Excellence and Faculty Development (TEFD) office. The Fall 2018 students in Comm 335: Media & Education were unintentional participants in the development of this text; thank you for your energetic conversations that propelled many of these ideas. My stupendous colleagues make every day a fun adventure. Aaron Hoholik and Marianne Neal-Joyce are stellar advisors; our students are lucky to have you both in their corner. Omadelle Nelson, Jackie Brousseau-Pereira, Erica Scharrer, and Alesia Brennan are incredible women with profound strength of character who always put a smile on my face. To work with a woman as insightful as Omadelle Nelson is a gift; the Department is stronger because of you. Jackie Brousseau-Pereira is an enthusiastic friend, neighbor, colleague, sage, and one of the most driven and hard-working women I know. Erica Scharrer is too many things to mention; the short list includes friend, colleague, confidante, and inspiration. Getting through the week would be way less manageable were it not for Wednesday evenings with Alesia Brennan.

I am honored to work with some serious intellectual giants in the media literacy world. Much of this work was inspired by the research and scholarship of David Buckingham, who has been so generous with his time, talking through ideas and sharing stories. In my work with ACME and MFF, I thank Andrea Bergstrom, Lori Bindig, Ben Boyington, Jacques Brodeur, Julie Frechette, Gordon Glover, Nolan Higdon, Mickey Huff, Andy Lee Roth, Sherell McArthur, and Bill Yousman for friendship and professional camaraderie. This group of people is changing the world in incredible ways. Thank you to Bill Reynolds who encouraged me to run with this research and brought me into the Brill organization. Thanks to the well-organized and timely editors at Brill, especially Jolanda Karada and Evelien van der Veer, as well as the kind and incisive words of the anonymous reviewers of the first draft. Special thanks to Ben Boyington for reading an early, sloppy draft. Extra special thanks to Nolan Higdon for being an amazing colleague, for reading early drafts, and for exploring both ideas and cities with me. Nolan, you are a solid compatriot and a dear friend; thank you so very, very much.

A crew of incredible women keep me grounded. I am a better person because of them. I've known and loved Lisa Green, Chris Heller, and Sherry Stregack more years than not; 30+years of friendship is no joke, ladies. Lev Ben-Ezra, Kat Good-Schiff, and Jen Good-Schiff share more adventures than can be detailed. Thank you for friendship, mountain climbing, rock climbing, and sisterhood. Alesia Brennan, what an amazing and inspiring woman you are; I admire your strength, tear-inducing sense of humor, and grace. Erica Scharrer, I'm where I am because of your support. Mindy Cotherman put a roof over our heads and then started fixing it – thank you, Mindy, for your expertise in so many things! There are some pretty fabulous men in my life, too, who respect women and counter the current face of toxic masculinity. Jake Artz and Nolan Higdon, I'm thinking of you both. Without all of you, my life would be missing a whole lot of love, laughter, and adventure.

I'm blessed to have a rich family of origin and family of destination. My siblings Stephanie, Andrew, Jennifer, and Christopher and in-laws Jim and Jennifer are wonderful human beings, outshined only by their even more fantastic kids. I thoroughly enjoy watching Jacob, Jasmin, Sarah, Eva, Charlotte, Annabelle, and Madeline grow up as curious, inquisitive human beings. Caro, as the '6th kid,' you are a gift: The little sister I never had, a wonderful soul, and a beacon of good humor. The Ben-Ezra, Lobenstine, and Whittington families are such a rich part of my life: My step-son Steve, in-laws, cousins, aunts, uncles, nieces, nephews, and so on – I'm deeply enamored. Alysia, Ted, Aviva, and Zale continue to inspire me and warm my heart with their endless capacity for love.

This book was written in the aftermath of the death of my father, a gifted writer and wordsmith. His precisely detailed accounts of military and naval history are important publications, but it was his writing to us – holiday poems, riddles to unlock passwords, and detailed notes scratched in carefully organized notebooks – that are among my fondest memories. My father was my toughest critic and always expected me to work harder and get the point across more clearly. I hope I've done him justice on these and any future pages. In the months since my father's death, extended time with my mother has been soul-enriching. She is the strongest human being on the planet and I hope that I have absorbed enough of her teaching to be half the woman she is. Much of this book was written and revised at her dining room table and I'm forever grateful for our quality time together.

And last but certainly not least: So much love to my two best guys. Andy, you are my rock; I love you more than words. Sancho, you are a dog, which means you cannot read. I have no doubt, however, that you know you are the love of my life and my absolute best friend in the world. I would be lonely and less whole without you both. My heart and soul are richer because of you two.

CHAPTER 1

Education Is the Answer (What Is the Question?)

Abstract

This chapter argues that work in media literacy is a necessary part of education because it can foster the space for a more thoroughly informed and involved citizenry. The chapter details the main argument of the text, that education in media literacy needs to begin with teachers, preferably during their formal schooling. This chapter shares the foundational definition of media literacy and argues that more specifically, teachers deserve education in *critical* media literacy, with its attention to structures of power.

1 Introduction

Almost without fail, for generations of time, 'school' and 'education' have been the standard, all-encompassing generic answer, even when the specificity of a question went unasked. Education was presented as the primary tool for civilizing mankind in the 16th and 17th centuries (Locke, 1693/2011; Rousseau, 1962/2011), the answer for women's liberation in the 18th century (Wollstonecraft, 1792/2011), racial equality in the 19th century (Anderson & Summerfield, 2004), and combatting communism in the 20th century (Ravitch, 1983). Coinciding with a time of rapid digital change, education in the 21st century is tasked with preparing students for jobs that do not yet exist (Darling-Hammond, 2010).

Simultaneously, 21st century students are part of the most media saturated society in human history. As of 2010, 8–18-year-olds fill 10 hours and 45 minutes of media use into a seven-hour and 38-minute time frame (Kaiser Family Foundation, 2010). That is, they multitask their usage, using multiple media at one time. High media use cuts across gender, race, and class (Anderson & Jiang, 2018; Kaiser Family Foundation), with African-American and Hispanic youth using media about 13 hours a day (Kaiser Family Foundation). As of 2018, 95% of United States' teenagers reported owning or having access to a smartphone, up from 73% in 2014–2015 (Anderson & Jiang, 2018). 45% of United States' teenagers say they are online on a near constant basis, up from 24% in 2014–2015 (Anderson & Jiang, 2018). 97% of United States' boys report playing video games (Anderson & Jiang, 2018). While self-reported data may

© KONINKLIJKE BRILL NV, LEIDEN, 2020 | DOI: 10.1163/9789004416765_001

be exaggerated, it nevertheless is quite clear that a great variety of media are available to, and consumed by, young people today. Even if these self-reports of home or personal use are exaggerated, young people have access to a variety of media and technologies outside the home (Schofield-Clark, 2014). As of 2010, 74% of United States' 7–12th graders have a social media profile (Kaiser Family Foundation, 2010). Only three in 10 youth report having any family-imposed time limits on their media use (Kaiser Family Foundation, 2010).

How media are used is changing. For example, by 2010, television viewing *on* television had decreased by 25 minutes, but had increased on mobile media (Kaiser Family Foundation, 2010). 'How' does not always correlate with 'what' and, as Buckingham (2007) points out, 'new' media build on established tropes of 'old' media, so distinguishing between the two may make little sense. That is, many of us are regularly surrounded by media and, increasingly there is less incentive to employ an 'off' switch.

Generally speaking, young people are audience to mainstream media, which is becoming sharply consolidated into a small number of extraordinarily powerful corporations. Media ownership has consolidated significantly in the 21st century with six corporate owners responsible for 90% of media content[1] (P. Phillips, 2018; PBS, 2017). This number shows it is clear it is a small number of conglomerates who "provide an international language or 'common culture,' particularly among young people" (Buckingham, 2007, pp. 81–82). Despite access to a great quantity of outlets, the content is relatively limited and regularly repeated. Americans mostly learn about United States' interests (Shah, 2012; Project for Excellence in Journalism, 2008), which may result in audiences being broadly informed about a small quantity of national issues and largely uninformed about global issues.

While the 'Big 6' refer to corporations with significant media content as part of their holdings, digital powerhouses are increasing their claim on media platforms and content. In August 2018, Apple became a $1 trillion company with stocks trading above $207 a share (DeRousseau, 2018). Close on Apple's heels are Amazon at $872 billion, Google's parent company Alphabet at $844 billion, Microsoft at $816 billion, and Facebook at $504 billion (DeRousseau). While many people may struggle to map out the myriad corporate connections among media conglomerates, Apple, Amazon, Google, and Facebook are all familiar names and companies with whom everyday users might feel a relatively close connection (M. Phillips, 2018). Today, 30 companies, led by the above four, receive half the profits of all publicly traded companies (M. Phillips, 2018). 'Trillion dollar company' is not without historical precedent; at its height, translated to today's dollars, the Dutch East India Trading Company was an $8.2 trillion company (DeRousseau).

EDUCATION IS THE ANSWER (WHAT IS THE QUESTION?)

Who has access to what media has long been a concern of media scholars. This concern of the 'digital divide' is re-imagined in the early 21st century. Whereas it was previously understood that the poor had limited access to technology – and thereby were at a disadvantage for professional advancement – the new imagining of that divide is wealthy parents with access to the latest technologies who limit their children's use for fear of addiction and behavioral problems (Bowles, 2018b). It is a divide structured by privilege rather than lack of access. High-level Silicon Valley tech developers report they do not let their children use the technologies they invent because they are aware of their addictive properties (Bowles, 2018a). In an ironic twist, poor youth may have greater screen access and make more use of screens because their parents/guardians are not exposed to the literature warning against excess screen time. While this might be seen as beneficial for tech-related job training, it further penalizes economically struggling young people who do not have a variety of activities to choose from as ways to spend their leisure time. Media and technology use remain a form of childcare and in economically stressed households and/or single-parent homes, technology use by children may present an option for the parent/guardian to get household responsibilities completed with minimal distractions or additional costs (Schofield-Clark, 2014).

Quantity of time spent with media and access to a quantity of technologies contribute to how we see the world and through what lens. Livingstone (2018) writes:

> The more media mediate everything in society – work, education, information, civic participation, social relationships and more – the more vital it is that people are informed about and critically able to judge what's useful or misleading, how they are regulated, when media can be trusted, and what commercial or political interests are at stake.

Quantity of time spent and quantity of media accessed does not automatically translate to behavioral changes. The quantity of time and available technology does beg the question: What do we know about that which we (potentially) spend so much time? More specifically, what do young people know about that which they are primed to spend so much time?

2   Main Argument

I argue throughout this text that work in media literacy is a necessary part of education because it can foster the space for a more thoroughly informed and involved citizenry. Media literacy does not operate on its own, however. The key argument in this text is that education in media literacy needs to begin with teachers, preferably during their formal schooling. This book is a manifesto for the inclusion of media literacy in teacher education and, by extension, in K-12 classrooms. Media literacy is necessary for today's teachers and should be part of their education. Courses in media literacy need to be woven into prospective teachers' education across the curriculum, not just in one-off workshops or professional development opportunities; it should be integrated into their curriculum and certification preparation so that they can, in turn, integrate into their curriculum development and lesson plans. More specifically, as defined and discussed in Chapters 2, 5, and 6, I argue that prospective teachers deserve education in *critical* media literacy, with its attention to structures of power.

This text addresses two apparently disparate topics – teacher education and media literacy – and illustrates how they are actually intertwined. The United States struggles with how best to train and retain prospective teachers. Simultaneously, the United States struggles with how to make better understanding of the mainstream media that occupies a significant amount of the populace's time and energy. These two struggles can join forces and make inroads towards a solution through the following: The inclusion of critical media literacy in teacher education programs.

Both critical media literacy and teacher education suffer the burden of being complex processes for which a surfeit of simple solutions are offered. Both education and media feel familiar to many people, so reason dictates the solutions to their problems must be easily graspable. Those of us who have received a comprehensive education may implicitly believe that we know how to teach because we've had, on average, 12–16 years of teachers, good, bad, memorable, or forgotten. The romantic, idyllic notion of teaching as a way to bond with young people in shared intellectual pursuit and soft-focus solutions to social problems proffered by mainstream media representations may bear no resemblance to the lived experiences of teachers. In his study of social justice and teacher education Keiser (2005) writes:

> A TV show cannot portray the challenging, tedious reality of schools and also maintain high ratings. And neither can policy makers, including the U.S. Department of Education, easily present the complexities of education without confusing the public. But rather than embrace and promote the dynamic complexity of teaching and learning, they instead promote simplistic reductions with rhetorical pronouncements and little cohesion. (p. 32)

It is the argument of this book that including critical media literacy as part of teacher education can and will solve problems. By learning more about how the media operate and how so much of our world knowledge is learned and filtered through the media, the classroom experience for teachers and students can be more relevant, creating a space for students to be active in their learning and teachers to create curriculum that bridges subject learning with engaged participation.

Despite being the largest producer and distributor of media around the globe, the United States struggles in its education about the media. United States' scholars have been concerned with the study of the media since the early days of newspaper, radio and TV, however, it was not until the early 1990s that 'media literacy' – as a term and as an object of study – was codified in the United States. The Aspen Institute defines media literacy as:

> ... hands-on and experiential, democratic (the teacher is researcher and facilitator) and process-driven. Stressing as it does critical thinking, it is inquiry-based. Touching as it does on the welter of issues and experiences of daily life, it is interdisciplinary and cross-curricular. (Aufderheide, 1993, p. 2)

In the 30 years since this codification, there have been great strides in media literacy inclusion in the United States, but these strides have largely been found in individual classrooms, by individual teachers, in community programs, or in one-time training programs. This attention has not changed the systemic challenges felt in the United States in bringing media literacy to greater structural inclusion.

A major obstacle to media literacy inclusion in classrooms is the state-based organization of public schools in the United States with little federal oversight (Kubey, 1998). If a single school, school district, or even state is interested in including media literacy, there are no commonly shared curricular guides, federal expectations, or resources. Teachers, administrators, and schools are on their own, left to their own devices.

Public discussion of media literacy generally receives positive attention – no one will state that *illiteracy* is a viable option – but the lack of actual inclusion leaves the positive, progressive language empty of any muscle. Since the contentious 2016 presidential election, there has been an increased interest in media literacy, but there is little cohesion as to where or how to include the training and no systematic structure or funding for training has been established. Private corporations make inroads into media literacy through financial contribution or technology contributions (coupled with thinly veiled user guides masked as curriculum), but I will argue that these options are dangerous if media literacy wishes to remain independent of corporate control.

Schooling, with well-trained teachers, can be the site of profound social change. According to Buckingham (2007), "Obviously, the school is not about to disappear. Yet in an environment that is increasingly dominated by the proliferation of electronic media and the demands of consumer culture, it urgently needs to assume a much more proactive role" (p. 183). If teachers and prospective teachers are educated in critical media literacy, it becomes *part of*, not *an addition to*, their regular lesson planning. I am not asking teachers and prospective teachers to add *more* to their already full plates. Instead, I am asking that comprehensive, university-based teacher education include critical media literacy in the core curricula, in order to prepare the most well-trained teachers to face current and future challenges in the classroom.

There is a conspicuous absence of media literacy education in classrooms and a formal approach to inclusion, via legislation, is often so weakly worded or so buried in other bills, as to be rendered ineffective. For example, proposed bills in various states all encourage media literacy or, more broadly, digital literacy, but with no mandated requirements. New Mexico was the first state to propose the legislation of media literacy in classrooms, beginning in 2009. The language of the bill was refined over the years and at its strongest, the bill stated that media literacy "shall be offered as an elective" (Public school media literacy classes, 2009). "Elective" implies that it is not necessary and "shall be offered" is not required. This is, at best, an invitation that can be ignored. In Massachusetts, the media literacy bill (An act concerning media literacy, 2013) was bundled into a civic engagement bill and shrank from detailing what was needed down to one phrase – "concerning media literacy" – in the absorbed bill (An act to involve youth in civic engagement, 2014). In New Jersey, the proposed media literacy bill states that "the department of education shall encourage each board of education to offer instruction in media literacy" but with no explanation of how this will be done ("An act concerning the teaching of media literacy," 2014). Similar to the language in New Mexico, "encourage" is not a requirement. Sometimes bills are responsive to particular concerns, such as California's bill to include computer science to the STEM curriculum, to prepare students for a digital workspace (California State Legislature, 2013). Reacting to a problem or concern is helpful, but it is neither predictive nor proactive and does not set up a sustainable frame for future work. Without funded mandates or any semblance of requirement, media literacy inclusion will languish.

3 Media Literacy: Foundations

While the United States is the largest producer and exporter of mass media products, it was not an early adopter of media literacy. Industrialized, Western nations outside the United States – especially the United Kingdom, Canada, and Australia – began their formal training in and learning of media literacy much earlier than the United States (Domaille & Buckingham, 2001; Tyner, 2015). This happened, in part, because these other countries were defending their population against the influx of American media (Buckingham, 1998b). Jhally and Earp (2003) point out that because work in media literacy spends so much time reacting to conservative attacks, "media literacy professionals spend a lot of time justifying themselves" (p. 24). This means that much work in media literacy in the United States is talking *about* media literacy rather than *doing* media literacy and, even more problematically, bickering about whether what has already been done is valid (Hobbs, 2011b; Potter, 2010).

Buckingham's (2003, 2007) definition of media literacy and approach to media literacy is a standard-bearer in the field. Buckingham (2003) defines media *education* as the "process of teaching and learning about media," with media *literacy* as "the outcome – the knowledge and skills learners acquire" (p. 4). Media literacy involves a combination of analysis and production, "'writing' the media as well as 'reading' them" (Buckingham, 2007, p. 163). If *education* is the answer to a host of social struggles, Buckingham refines the answer further: *Media education* is the answer to multiple pedagogical and social questions, including how to understand the mainstream media's role in both the larger culture as well as in young people's lives, how to understand and talk back to the power of market forces, and how to address what young people know, enjoy, and struggle with in their media choices. To be media literate is not to possess a finite set of skills, but rather to have working knowledge of, and knowledge to apply, key concepts (Bazalgette, 1992; Buckingham, 2003, 2007). By working through concepts, teaching and learning of media literacy can be flexible with content and adaptable to changing and uses of technologies.

In the early 1980s, Masterman (1980, 1985) began discussing media literacy learning as a series of concepts. A concepts-based approach invites a level of flexibility and is less subjective to the whims, trends, and fluctuations of technologies and content. A concepts-based approach moves beyond a limited set of skills or tools. Masterman's (1985) work, while valuable, was rooted in the notion media literacy work would 'demystify' students' engagement and experience with the media. This implicitly reinforced the belief that young people were 'mystified' by the mainstream media. Furthermore, Masterman presented the classroom study of media as a simple transference of theory to practice: The ideas he presented and lessons he constructed could be seamlessly woven into the classroom. Masterman (1980) realized that his students were not watching as many movies as he anticipated, but by tweaking his examples to TV – the medium of choice at the time of his work – the formula for media analysis would be clear. He did not draw attention to what young people already knew and what knowledge they brought to the classroom space. While the classroom work would draw on student conversation, the teacher remained the primary leader and (presumed) possessor of knowledge. Even with young people's participation, media literacy learning would be a simple transference of data from teacher to student. A problem with this is it limits student participation to classroom-appropriate "right" and "wrong" answers and may limit the relevancy of media examples.

Acknowledging the complexities of the classroom space, awareness of the difficulties of theories applied to practice, and addressing what young people bring to the conversation, Bazalgette (1992), Grahame (1991), and Buckingham (1990, 1993a, 1998b), changed the shape of media literacy in the United Kingdom and had massive influence around the globe. Buckingham (1990), Buckingham and Sefton-Green (1994), and Buckingham, Grahame and Sefton-Green's (1995) empirical work in classrooms emphasized that bringing media studies to primary and secondary school classrooms was more complicated than initially anticipated while Grahame's (1991) work illustrated the value of youth production as a key site of learning.

No neat and tidy write-up or well-constructed argument could accurately reflect the challenges of media learning in classrooms. Teachers often work in isolation with little institutional or administrative support or additional resources (Buckingham, 1990; Buckingham, Fraser, & Mayman, 1990; Buckingham & Sefton-Green, 1994). Including popular culture in classroom work can reveal a teacher's lack of knowledge or appreciation of content, which must be met with a willingness to learn from students. The classroom immersed in media literacy is student-centered and responsive to student-interest. The teacher is a facilitator, not the sole transmitter of data. The inclusion of popular culture means classrooms need to be flexible to address a variety of texts. Because students often come to classrooms with an awareness of expected behavior, work in media learning often involves breaking down the necessity of a 'right' answer, leaving classroom discussions more fluid, but also less controlled. Teachers must have a degree of comfort moving beyond their own repertoire of data.

Media literacy work can expose the fault lines in a classroom or school because of its attention to representation and power. When young people are granted the opportunity to critique their surroundings, they may very well critique their teachers, classrooms, and communities. Space may be made for students to vocalize critiques that may not 'fit' with classroom expectations – with the knowledge that students may or may not make their critiques explicit. Analysis of how young people make sense of the media may reveal their own biases and may teach them about themselves. Teachers can incorporate these critiques through an exploration of content within its larger context. The question, of course, is whether teachers will abdicate authority. One can be an authority without being overly authoritative: Invite students to bring in their own texts and to share their own experiences, wherein the teacher operates as facilitator rather than primary voice. It is equally as likely that young people will be suspicious of a classroom discussion of their media choices, assuming that they will be taught the media, and by extension, their interests, are bad. Young people may initially resent media learning, especially if it is presented in a negative manner. This may prove to be too threatening to school communities, but it need not be. Self and systemic reflection may ultimately make students and schools better informed and better equipped to make change.

What Buckingham and colleagues did that was so valuable at the time – and remains so – is to acknowledge what young people already know, before entering the classroom. Young people do not come to classrooms as empty vessels; they have a great deal of colloquial knowledge and opinions about many topics, including various media. When the study of the media is brought to classrooms, young people are savvy enough as students that they know the 'right' answer, in terms of classroom decorum, even if they are unaware of the specific content. It takes tremendous practice to be able to critique the media while simultaneously acknowledge enjoyment of them. Including media literacy as part of the curriculum may break down the long-held traditional belief of teacher/authority, student/supplicant. It provides young people greater autonomy over and authority of their learning. It invites students to bring their interests to the classroom, thereby creating the space to connect them more fully to their coursework and invites students and teachers to work together. It is also important to acknowledge that 'what young people know' includes the assumed-appropriate classroom behavior and students may reject the inclusion of 'their' interests under suspicion that they might be overly criticized. Including media literacy as part of the curriculum also demands a great deal of patience.

Scholarship in the United Kingdom in the late 1980s began to develop the notion of conceptual learning. First iterated by Masterman (1985), the mantle was picked up and made more nuanced by Bazalgette (1992) who articulated six key aspects of media learning. These aspects – agency, category, technology, language, audience, and representation – were constructed as ways to address the study of the media in a way that involved students directly in the process. Conceptual learning breaks open the teacher-student hierarchy, invites students into an autonomous relationship with their learning, highlights their expertise and interests, and is non-trendy, enabling a greater flexibility with changes in content and technology.

Bazalgette's (1992) six key aspects of media education have been refined to four key concepts: production, language, representation, and audience (Buckingham, 2003). Discussed in detail in Buckingham (2003), in brief, these four concepts cover the following:

> *Production:* Media texts are consciously manufactured. Addressing production asks questions about how the media are constructed and for what purpose.
>
> *Language:* Visual and spoke languages communicate meaning; familiar codes and conventions make meaning clear.
>
> *Representation:* Events are made into stories which invite audiences to see the world in one way and not in others.
>
> *Audience:* Explores who is engaging with what texts and how people are targeted. (pp. 53–67)

The key concepts provide a way to organize classroom practices, systematically approach the study of a variety of texts, provide teachers and students questions to ask of any material, and can be easily adapted to changes in technology. While the concepts can be treated as unique entities, they are best understood as a complex whole with multiple interlocking parts. Media literacy concepts invite dynamic, rather than static, learning, opens up the conversation to include what young people already know about the media, and draws on their knowledge and enjoyment of media texts. The concepts are non-trendy and are flexible enough to expand to include changes in technology and the location of media use. Buckingham (2007) updated the concepts to include questions of digital media:

> *Representation:* Explores authority, reliability, and bias; looks at whose stories are told and whose are ignored.
>
> *Language:* Digital literacy looks at digital rhetoric, especially website design and links.
>
> *Production:* Explores the 'invisible' commercialization of digital media and global role of advertising, promotion, and sponsorship.
>
> *Audience:* Looks at how users access sites, how they are guided through sites, and the role of users' data gathering. (pp. 155–156)

EDUCATION IS THE ANSWER (WHAT IS THE QUESTION?)

The United States regularly debates the merits of media content and representation but struggles with reflection and analysis of mainstream media practices. When the 'Big 6' United States'-based multinational conglomerates (P. Phillips, 2018) own, produce and distribute the vast majority of media content, all media are 'local' and American audiences are not threatened or intimidated by 'foreign,' imported media. United States media are presented as ubiquitous and naturally occurring; young people in the United States need not question why the media are the way they are because they do not need to comb through 'other'/foreign options to find familiar content of their choosing. Especially in a time of increased mobile media, when 'everything' feels so easily accessible, the incentive for questioning the means of production is diluted.

While it is agreed upon that media literacy is important, there is little to no agreement on where to include it or how 'best' to teach it. Schools are already full to bursting with content and curricular expectations (Kubey, 1998; Jenkins, Purushotma, Clinton, Weigel, & Robinson, 2006). In this void, private enterprises rush in (Giroux, 2007; Harvey, 2005; Klein, 2007) and maneuver public systems into private interests. Private interests and for-profit schooling are presented as streamlined solutions, but this presentation masks the reality that funding is pulled from public schools, teachers are often offered minimal support, students and families must fight for attention, and, maybe most importantly, there is no compelling evidence that these models work. Meanwhile, in public schools, an overemphasis on testing limits opportunities for other subjects, electives, and subjects deemed non-academic are easily cancelled in the face of restrictive budgets and limited resources. Essential to the work of media literacy is the emphasis on mainstream media's inherent commercial priority (Jhally & Earp, 2003); the mainstream media in the United States are private, for-profit companies. Our entertainment and pleasure is second, maybe, to their number one priority: Profit. The perceived ease of access of mainstream media, especially in this digital era when so much of what we watch, read, or listen to can be instantly available on our laptops or tablets and, more immediately, in our pockets, on digital devices, lulls us into believing they need not be studied.

4   Focus of the Book

This text is focused primarily on United States' K-12 public education. About 50.7 million young people attend public schools (Back to school statistics, n.d.) versus 5.9 million who attend private school (Back to school statistics, n.d.; Fast Facts, n.d.). 78% of parents who send their children to the neighborhood public school self-report this is a choice they are happy with (Cookson,

Darling-Hammond, Rothman, & Shields, 2018). There are approximately 3.2 million full-time public school teachers, with an average student/teacher ratio of 16 to 1 (Back to school statistics, n.d.). In 2018, approximately $12,910 was spent per public school student (Back to school statistics, n.d.). Approximately 19.9 million people attend college/university, down slightly from the 2010 peak of 21 million (Back to school statistics, n.d.). Of those 19.9 million, 12.3 million will be under the age of 25 years and 69.8% will enroll in college immediately after graduating high school (Back to school statistics, n.d.). There are approximately 98,300 public schools in the United States, which includes about 6900 charter schools (Back to school statistics, n.d.). Public schooling and its progression from K-12 through college is a major aspect of life in America, yet it remains largely unclear and hotly contested.

The 'public' of public schooling is under threat and has been for decades. Neoliberalism, the economic philosophy that emphasizes the free market and hyper-individualism, worked its way into public education via Milton Friedman (1955) and his interest in education. When Friedman first proposed the idea of vouchers and school choice as a means to dismantle government (public) schooling, of which he was opposed, he started a backlash against public schools. This backlash grew stronger in 1983 with the publication of *A Nation at Risk*, which stated that American schoolchildren were falling dangerously behind their global peers. Since the 1980s, there has been increased private interest in schooling, especially in ways to make money from the process of schooling children. Buckingham (2011) writes:

> Schooling – and education more broadly – is an increasingly important arena for children's encounters with consumer culture. Many key aspects of what was formerly public educational provision – from school buildings and facilities to teacher training and examinations – are now provided and run by private companies. (p. 204)

The current fight against public schools involves billionaire business people donating massive amounts of money to election campaigns of candidates in favor of charter schools and opposed to unions (Strauss, 2014; The Network for Public Education [NPE], 2018). Currently, significantly fewer young people attend charter schools than attend public schools, but the numbers of charter school enrollments are on a rapid rise (Cookson et al., 2018) and charter school development is praised as a panacea to the (perceived) quagmire of public schooling.

We live in a time when public institutions and social services are under threat of neoliberalism which works to privatize and compartmentalize public works in favor of private interest. Despite attention paid to private education organizations and rapid development of charter schools, public schools in the United States are still a fundamental part of democracy. Public schooling may be the one institution capable of rescuing itself and other public institutions from the destructive properties of neoliberalism. Public school teachers and public school students are in a unique position to make change and fight back against neoliberalism – but they cannot do it alone. Public schooling is, admittedly, deeply flawed and needs actual, radical reform. This reform and the needed support can be found in media literacy, specifically in bringing media literacy training into teacher education.

5 Conclusion

In November 2018, the *New York Times* published an exposé on a high school in Louisiana that falsified massive amounts of student data in order to ensure acceptance into highly selective colleges (Green & Benner). By June 2019, the *New York Times'* docuseries *The Weekly*, about the student whistleblowers, debuted on FX and Hulu. Based on the *New York Times'* investigation into the school, the FBI is looking into the school's college admissions practices (Benner & Green, 2019). This story encapsulates much of what is the matter with alternative schooling, teachers without systemic support, students and families with minimal cultural capital, and our own desire to believe that education is the unilateral exit route from poverty.

T.M. Landry College Preparatory School, in Beaux Bridge, Louisiana falsified the transcripts of its largely black, working class student body. The Landry School is private and non-accredited. The state does not recognize its diploma, though the school does follow Louisiana state standards. Parents were promised a substantive education, but struggled to see the value or depth of their children's curriculum. Students were encouraged to falsify or exaggerate difficult childhoods, submitting personal essays that played into and exploited minority stereotypes: Absentee fathers, negligent parents, and poverty-stricken communities, for example. The school was founded by Michael and Tracey Landry, two people with negligible pedagogical experience – Tracey was a nurse and Michael was a teacher and a salesman – who credited teachers and schooling with helping them escape poverty. In the exposé, the Landrys are accused of physically abusing and berating students.

Videos of students opening their college acceptance letters have gone viral on social media and Landry students have been profiled on national television shows, including *The Today Show*, *Ellen*, and CBS *Morning News*. This exposure led to money being sent to the school to support students and pressure was put upon the Landrys to open more schools. The money sent to the school was never spent on students in any clear way. The Landrys allegedly threatened and intimidated students and their families, convincing them the school was their only route to college and that they could support or sabotage the process for the students. Upon publication of the exposé, the Landry School is still open and enrolling students.

This story holds a mirror up to our ugly relationship with education. The widespread media attention and viral videos make the rest of us feel better about education and serve as 'evidence' both that public schooling is incapable of change because of its overly bureaucratic construction and that individuals are responsible for their own success. The college acceptances boost the diversity statistics of elite, largely white, institutions. The national TV coverage purports to illustrate that 'regular' people matter.

However, paying attention to this story as a singular narrative of success or struggle masks a bigger structural concern: These young people and this school are part of a larger system that needs attention. In a response to the *New York Times* exposé, Gerald (2018) reminds readers that while the T.M. Landry School is indeed a tragic example of academic power gone awry, it cannot be viewed as a "singular, extraordinary case of fraud and abuse perpetrated by two villains" (nytimes.com). Gerald reminds us we must look at the larger system which regularly fails students. While the outliers – both successful and struggling – are important, it is the larger system which needs much closer examination, especially to peel away the layers that neoliberalism has built, convincing those with privilege and those who struggle that it is up to them, alone, to succeed or fail. Upon college enrollment, most Landry alumni found themselves struggling academically and suffering from mental health crises, especially anxiety and depression, because the falsifications and lack of actual education preparation caught up to them. They fell into patterns that Gerald writes are all too common for underserved young people: Being told for so long that education is the only 'way out,' but not being provided enough resources to make the 'exit.'

Better teacher education and media literacy will not prevent this story or others like it from happening. It will not undo the mental and physical crises experienced by these students. It cannot hold the Landrys legally responsible for their choices.

However, better teacher education, including media literacy, can serve, over time, to bolster public schooling. Media literate students, teachers, and families may have greater ability to approach the flashy promises of alternative education and alternative teacher education. They may explore individual stories within a broader context, interrogating the system as well as the story.

EDUCATION IS THE ANSWER (WHAT IS THE QUESTION?)   15

If public schooling is stronger, more families may not feel the need to seek alternative routes to education. If media literacy is part of teacher education and, by extension, part of K-12 schooling, high school graduates will possess greater access to critical thinking and critical assessments, which may alter the progression of society. Media literacy enfolded into teacher education is not a short-term solution and it is not a flashy solution to educational struggles. Work in critical media literacy will most likely not go viral on social media and will not make scintillating copy on the morning shows or national talk shows. It will, however, make the United States academically stronger and more prepared for informed participation in civil society.

This book is organized in a way to support readers on a journey. Change is clearly needed and the change needs to be different from, not just a variation on, what has been done before. Public schooling *is* flawed, but at its foundation, is an admirable project. It is a public responsibility to educate the populace well, making them active citizens who participate in and give back to the community. A strong public school can build a strong public sphere. Let us not destroy public schooling for the tantalizing promises of the market (promises that, more often than not, are not realized). Instead, let us really, truly heal public schools through a new, radical, and totally feasible effort.

This effort's plausibility is traced in the journey of the following pages. The journey will begin by introducing media literacy and asking why it is important. Chapter 2 maps the environment of media literacy in the United States and provides an articulation of critical media literacy. It sets the stage for why media literacy is important and highlights the major gap in media literacy inclusion: Comprehensive teacher education.

What does it mean to be a K-12 teacher in the United States and why does it matter? Chapters 3 and 4 trace the history and struggles of teacher education in the United States and the various political struggles found in advancing a public school agenda in a country with a combination of state and federal school controls and policies that increasingly falls prey to free market promises.

How can the gap be filled? Chapter 5 makes the argument that despite the complications, now is the time to include critical media literacy into formal, university-based teacher education programs. Chapter 5 illustrates ways critical media literacy can be brought into teacher education and provides examples of how critical media literacy can be integrated across subject matters. The concluding chapter illustrates how media literacy can be worked into classes and details how the current tensions of school reform can be illustrated more clearly through media literacy analysis. Chapter 6 also discusses what critical media literacy looks like and how to distinguish 'good' from weak or corporate-connected efforts at media literacy.

Note

1 The 'Big 6' are, as of this writing: Comcast (major holdings: NBC, Universal Pictures); NewsCorp (major holdings: Fox, *Wall Street Journal*); Disney (major holdings: ABC, ESPN, Pixar); Viacom (major holdings: MTV, Nickelodeon, Paramount Pictures); Time Warner (major holdings: CNN, HBO, *Time*); and CBS (major holding: Showtime). Additional corporations include Yahoo!, Microsoft, and Google.

CHAPTER 2

Critical Media Literacy

Abstract

This chapter illustrates the necessity of a new starting point for media literacy learning: In teacher education programs. Teachers educated in media literacy will be able to integrate the study of the media across their classroom work, which may serve to connect their subject matter more directly with students, can contribute to a student-centered classroom, and can engage students and teachers together in a project of social justice-focused change making. Specifically, this chapter defines critical media literacy and starts the discussion on why the attention to structures of power is needed as part of media literacy training.

1 Introduction

> The instrument can teach, it can illuminate; yes, and even it can inspire. But it can do so only to the extent that humans are determined to use it to those ends. Otherwise it's nothing but wires and lights in a box. There is a great and perhaps decisive battle to be fought against ignorance, intolerance and indifference. This weapon of television could be useful. (Murrow, 1958)

The penultimate paragraph of Murrow's speech to the Radio & Television News Association's 1958 conference, calling for a more mature approach to broadcasting and greater awareness of broadcasters' responsibilities to the public, speaks to the 21st century need for critical media literacy. Sixty years after his speech, Murrow's words are as relevant as ever, and can be extended to our current media technologies. Our media – no longer dominated by TV and radio broadcasting – can teach, they illuminate, and yes, they inspire. We absolutely must fight ignorance, intolerance, and indifference. Murrow called on the men of broadcasting to be more attentive to the serious work of media production. Today that call must be extended to media literacy (and must not be specifically to men), it is the tool with which we can work against ignorance, intolerance, and indifference. This remains a human responsibility; we must be determined to make change in order to improve our awareness. If we do

© KONINKLIJKE BRILL NV, LEIDEN, 2020 | DOI: 10.1163/9789004416765_002

not include critical media literacy into our repertoire of media understanding and education, we run the risk of being lulled into ignorance by the wires and lights.

This chapter illustrates the necessity of a new starting point for media literacy learning: In teacher education programs. Before prospective teachers enter classrooms, when they are engaged in their own learning, they should be equipped with the tools to offer effective critical media literacy pedagogy. This is vital in order to combat the rising tide of increased corporate media monopoly, to make greater sense of social media and its permutations, to better understand ourselves and our own media use, to better understand the world in which we live and all its complexities, largely learned via the media, to develop a better understanding of content and representation, and to have a more thorough understanding of the means of production, critical media literacy belongs in teacher education. Teachers educated in media literacy will be able to integrate the study of the media across their classroom work, which may serve to connect their subject matter more directly with students, can contribute to a student-centered classroom, and can engage students and teachers together in a project of social justice-focused change making. Teacher training in media literacy can put a stop to the nebulous conversations that end with the statement that media literacy matters, but provide no provisions for its sustained inclusion (Livingstone, 2018).

For decades there have been arguments that media literacy is necessary. This chapter does not refute or belabor those arguments. By this point in history, it is safe to assume that debate is settled: We need media literacy. The question remains: Where to begin? Livingstone (2018) writes:

> It seems the mere suggestion [of media literacy] is enough to deflect attention from the politically undesirable or practically-challenging. Media literacy, conveniently, is someone else's responsibility and they (teachers, experts in pedagogy, the Department of Education) are rarely present when 'fake news' or platform regulation or journalism standards or data exploitation are being discussed. (blogs.lse.ac.uk)

This chapter makes the case that the acute need is the inclusion of media literacy in teacher education. More specifically, this chapter argues for *critical* media literacy as part of teacher education: Media literacy that includes political economy and explicitly critiques power, illustrating how the media are connected to their (and our) larger context. Thus far, throughout Chapter 1, I used the term 'media literacy;' with the definition and discussion of critical media literacy in this chapter, I will be more specific in the application

CRITICAL MEDIA LITERACY

of this particular qualifier. Media literacy is incomplete without analysis that addresses the 'behind the scenes' of media work, including ownership, production, and distribution. When prospective and new teachers enter the classroom, with critical media literacy as part of their repertoire, they can integrate its concepts and questions into their curriculum development and lesson planning.

2   How Media Literate Are Young People?

In 2004, Livingstone wrote, "Evaluation is crucial to literacy: Imagine the world wide web user who cannot distinguish dated, biased, or exploitative sources, unable to select intelligently when overwhelmed by an abundance of information and services" (eprints/lse.ac.uk/107). Fast forward 12 years, add in the explosive increase in and popularity of social media sites, the public's experience with mass disinformation campaigns and fake news, plus the election of a statistically consistently unpopular president (FiveThirtyEight, 2018) with a devoted base of radically conservative constituents (Egan, 2018), and the media literacy landscape may be what Livingstone warned against.

Just after the contentious 2016 United States Presidential election, the Stanford History Education Group (SHEG) released the findings of their nearly two-year study on young people's ability to evaluate and interpret information found on the internet. In their summary of the research findings, the authors contend that one word – *bleak* – encapsulates their perspective on young people's analytic abilities (Wineberg, McGraw, Breakstone, & Ortega, 2016). Students ranging from middle school through college were unable to distinguish between news/information and advertisements, recognize point of view or bias, and were unaware of who owns or runs certain websites. Despite their supposed near-constant use of media and their perceived technological prowess, SHEG found that the overwhelming majority of young people did not know how to make sense of the media they used. Young people are aware of a great deal of media, they are savvy manipulators of various technologies (often simultaneously), and they make conscientious choices about content and medium, but they do not know how to analyze the 'behind the scenes' or means of production of their choices. While this is upsetting, it is not surprising; mainstream media are not designed to be analyzed or critically assessed and currently, schools and teachers are not educated in how to teach this material.

This is deeply concerning and is a clarion call for increased attention to the necessity of media literacy training. This chapter is not a demand for greater media literacy in classrooms – though that is, of course, necessary. Nor is it an admonition of young people's media use – though that could be a relatively easy argument to make. This chapter is also not a history of media literacy. There are solid, detailed histories of media literacy in the United States (Hoechsmann & Poyntz, 2012; Kellner & Share, 2007; Tyner, 1998; Yousman, 2016) and around the globe (Domaille & Buckingham, 2001) and this chapter does not purport to reinvent those histories. The discussion of media literacy is framed as a tension between defensiveness/protection and democratization/inclusion as a way to make space for the need for critical media literacy training for teachers and young people.

3   Defensiveness to Democratization/Protection to Celebration

A global leader in media education, David Buckingham (2003) discusses the progression of media literacy in the United Kingdom as one that moves from defensiveness to democratization. *Defensiveness* refers to the history of studying popular culture as a negative, harmful thing. This position ostensibly begins with Leavis and Thompson's (1933) analysis and tools for practice to critique mass media with the aim that once students were aware of the negativity, they would make 'better' (high-culture) choices. Post-World War II United Kingdom saw the rise of Cultural Studies and an approach to popular culture that saw it as more infused with everyday life. Drawing on the work of Williams (1958/1983, 1961) and Hoggart (1959), while early British Cultural Studies work still saw the media and popular culture as problematic, they were not seen as an 'other' or an addendum to young people's lives.

The media and popular culture were firmly entrenched as part of young people's world. The influential works of Hall and Whannell (1965), Hall and Jefferson (1976), Hebdige (1979), and McRobbie (1976) codified British Cultural Studies and provided an in-depth, critical, ethnographic exploration of young people's popular cultural choices as complex and rich. Growing in prominence in the 1970s, with great attention to cinema, *Screen* theory argued that young people needed a set of tools to critique popular culture in order to best understand its manipulative properties.

The leading outgrowth of this approach was Masterman's (1980, 1985) early work in media literacy. Masterman was an early proponent of breaking away from *Screen* theory's rigid structure and Leavis and Thompson's (1933) criticism, while nevertheless arguing that young people needed skills of analysis that would reveal media and popular culture's inherent negativity and manipulation. The process of demystification would enlighten young people into more appropriate choices.

CRITICAL MEDIA LITERACY

In the late 1980s, Buckingham (1990, 1993a; Buckingham & Sefton-Green, 1994) broke away from this position, arguing against demystification and the inherent negativity of the media. He posited that young people get a great deal of pleasure and enjoyment from media and popular culture and this pleasure and enjoyment deserves study. Media industries, while indeed problematic in content and exploitation of youth audiences, provide a way for young people to interact with and understand the world. The move towards *democratization* acknowledged that young people's social cultures and choices were both valid and worthy of study. The media are explored as *part of*, not *separate from*, young people's lives. In addition, as argued regularly by Buckingham (1993; Buckingham & Sefton-Green, 1994, 1998a), the study of young people and media should begin by exploring what young people already know about media. Young people come to the conversation on media analysis knowing more than for what they are given credit. Adults/teachers do not have all the knowledge about media and popular culture and cannot be the sole purveyors of media 'truth.' To engage in a demystification process is to assume adults have greater knowledge *because* they are adults and it is in their role *as* adults to inform young people of what the media are *really* trying to convey. Through a democratized approach, adults/teachers provide the framework for study, facilitate learning through the concepts and questions of media literacy, and invite young people into a dialogue of analysis.

A similar, but differently structured, divide exists in the development of the study of popular culture and media literacy in the United States. The United States' protectionist position resides in effects research that quantifies or presumes negative behavioral and cognitive changes in young people due to continued exposure to media (Potter, 2012) and arguments about the inherent immorality of media content, specifically with regards to depictions of sex, drugs, and violence (Brown, El-Toukhy, & Ortiz, 2014). Mid-to-late-20th century concerns revolved around young people's television consumption habits, especially violent programming, which was believed to stunt their development as productive members of society (Postman, 1985, 1994; Winn, 1977). The late 20th into the 21st century is marked by concerns with more interactive media, such as video games and, increasingly, social media (Bleakley, Vaala, Jordan, & Romer, 2014; Flanagin & Metzger, 2010; Livingstone, 2014; Mazzarella, 2008; Montgomery, 2007; Schofield-Clark, 2008).

In the United States, the most common iteration of classroom-based media literacy takes a protectionist stance. In this execution, adult authority figures generally teach about the media in a way that highlights their negative, problematic role (Brown, 1998; Buckingham, 1991; Halloran & Jones, 1992). Media enjoyment is checked at the classroom door for both teacher and student.

The grounding assumption is that once young people learn that the media are mostly bad, they will make the choice to turn them off. In its philosophy and intentions, protectionism is a defensive position that aims to advise young people into wiser, more sophisticated choices. If part of media literacy is to empower young people in their autonomy as audiences, the only empowerment available here is for young people to deny their own enjoyment and turn off the media, without actually learning much about them.

The protectionist position takes a narrow view of media and, in turn, imparts that onto students: The media are bad and young people are too intellectually naive to know any differently. Through the protectionist position, those in positions of authority impart their knowledge onto young people. By definition, those teaching from a protectionist position are perceived to be – or perceive themselves to be – above the negative influence of the media. There is reliance upon the hierarchy of age and assumptions of expertise: Teachers/authority figures know best and young people will learn from their authority. While there is no incontrovertible evidence that the media are the singular culprit causing negative behavior, blaming the media remains enticing. The simplicity of blaming the media serves two purposes: It provides an easy scapegoat while simultaneously masking the need for more serious, complex, and complicated conversations. To blame the media ends the conversation. To look for a more complex set of factors exposes multiple levels of mistreatment over generations of media use and may make the teacher/authority figure complicit in the struggle. To dig deeper into the means of production and our own culpability is to introduce a more complex set of factors that insist we slow down our analysis to make more complex sense of the multiple layers of meaning in any media text.

The United States' responded to protectionism with its polar opposite: A celebration of the media. The celebratory position argues that media are not inherently bad and that with analysis and creative production, young people will choose – or, preferably, create – 'good' media. Young people's analysis and use of media, especially interactive media such as computer games, is to be celebrated as a new and different approach to the use of media. The celebratory position separates its object of study from 'passive' media – such as watching TV or movies or listening to music – and concentrates on interactive media such as computer games, video games, social media, and young people's digital and mobile media participation. The celebratory position sees young people as inherently wise in their content choices and active in their media use. It assumes young people will choose interactive media and that these choices are inherently good (boyd, 2009, 2010, 2014; Hobbs, 1998, 2011). Young people's creativity is presumed to be natural and spontaneous, supported by technology (Buckingham, 2000).

CRITICAL MEDIA LITERACY

With its underlying assumption that all young people have the same access to any and all media of their choosing – or that benevolent corporate benefactors will provide access for classroom use – the celebratory position leaves out attention to social and economic divisions. Technology is understood to liberate young people, giving them a freedom hampered by traditional media (Buckingham, 2008). With its attention on individual access to and use of media, the celebratory position seamlessly supports market forces with positive attention paid to media largely owned, produced, and distributed by a small group of interconnected multinational corporations.

Although the protectionist and celebratory position are opposites of each other in their ideological positions, they may have more in common beneath the surface. Both emphasize the content of media with little to no discussion on how that content came to fruition. Both see that young people can be making 'better' choices if they had 'correct' information. What remains missing in much of United States' media literacy is any significant attention to the means of production. Neither seems capable of accepting young people's increased knowledge about media content without a corresponding behavioral change. In both positions, if young people choose *not* to turn off media or choose *not* to create media, has media literacy failed? Protectionism and celebration leave too many loose ends and I argue that critical media literacy – with an explicit emphasis on studying the systems of ownership, production, and distribution – is the most thorough approach to the study of the media.

4   Critical Media Literacy

Despite their differences, protectionism and celebration share an important commonality: They are both largely a-contextual, focused primarily on content and representation. When media are analyzed, it is often as independent texts, disconnected from their larger environment. For example, young people learn how to deconstruct an advertisement, which may include discussion of the specific brand, but does not extend to the company who produced the advertisement, the medium or technology where the advertisement is found, the differences between messages in different media, or who is in charge of the means of production of the advertisement. The ethics of the specific product or a larger conversation on the culture of consumption may be left out. Textual analysis runs the risk of leaving students despondent; they may learn to see complexity in a text, but until they also learn how that text came to fruition and what larger purpose it serves, their analytic skills are incomplete. Critical media literacy fills in these gaps.

Critical media literacy is inquiry-based, engages in critiques of ideology, and includes analyses of gender, race, class, and sexuality. Critical media literacy encourages analysis of dominant ideology and interrogation of the means of production. It is largely rooted in social justice, providing opportunities for action (Kellner & Share, 2007). Critical media literacy employs political economy to study mainstream and independent media, including questions of ownership, distribution, and production. It involves a close examination of power. Critical media literacy is not 'media bashing' and does not tell students what to think. Rather, critical media literacy invites students to "view media in a more informed way and consider alternative ways of thinking about the media they use" (Yousman, 2016, p. 372). Analyzing media and culture through the lens of critical media literacy pays attention to its larger context: Not just the message of the text, but how that message fits into the larger environment. Students of critical media literacy are encouraged to locate and learn about independent, non-corporate media to illustrate how stories are told in different ways when the means of production follow different routes. With an emphasis on social justice, students of critical media literacy are encouraged to take steps to make change in their communities and are taught how to get involved and to 'talk back' to their media choices. Critical media literacy guides students through a process of continuous critical inquiry regarding a wide variety of media texts and invites them to think beyond the content of dominant mainstream media choices. Critical media literacy challenges students to think beyond their comfort and pleasure with media and to regularly interrogate their choices.

The term 'critical' is often conflated with 'negative,' resulting in the impression that those who are critical of the media dislike it. Critical media literacy is not about media dislike, per se, or, more specifically, about trying to convince students to dislike the media. To be critical is to take a step away from media content/representation in order to examine its larger context. To be critical is to attempt to look at one's emotional connection to a particular text or technology not to belittle or disavow that emotional connection but rather, to explore under what circumstances that emotional connection got made.

While it shares intellectual roots, critical media literacy is not synonymous with critical theory. Drawing from Marxism, critical media literacy addresses questions of power, especially in its exploration and deconstruction of dominant ideology. Critical media literacy scholars may draw from approaches to cultural analysis articulated by Adorno (1991) and Horkheimer and Adorno (1947/2002). Critical media literacy draws from Althusser's (1970) deconstruction of dominant ideology and ideological states apparatuses. Critical media literacy scholars draw from Cultural Studies, especially its intersection of popular culture and audience research (McRobbie, 1976; Hebdige, 1979). Critical media literacy borrows from feminism in its exploration of unequal treatment and exploring that which has been ignored or mistreated in scholarship as well as media content (hooks, 1994; McRobbie, 1976). For critical media literacy scholars, this scholarship lineage may be part of their legacy of research. Critical media literacy's unique position is found in its hands-on work, coupled with analysis, by youth constituents. It is largely, but not exclusively, classroom-based, while, simultaneously, encourages young people to look at their worlds – including, but not exclusively, school – through a critical media lens. Critical media literacy's direct and consistent practical work brings theory to life and addresses young people's legitimacy as meaning-makers and critical thinkers.

There is a lot of talk in media literacy about the need for critical skills and media education has been tasked with making young people 'critical.' As Buckingham (2000b) points out, there is not always a clear definition of 'critical' or what difference being critical will make. He clarifies that critical judgment "needs to be regarded as a *discursive strategy* – that is, a form of social action which is intended to accomplish particular social purposes" (p. 212). Drawing from interviews with young people about their news watching, Buckingham (2000b) notes that youth responses must be contextualized; though they may speak 'critically' in interviews, they may behave differently outside the interview context. Buckingham (2003) notes, "Media education, it is argued, is fundamentally concerned with the development of 'critical consciousness' ... But what is meant by the term critical here? What distinguishes a 'critical' approach from one that is merely 'uncritical'?" (p. 107). The answer lies in autonomy. Young people may be savvy students and know how to produce the ideologically 'right' answer in class. Young people may know how to recognize what individual teachers want and what is expected of them by the larger system of schooling (even if they do not possess the skills to reach the answer(s)).

To be critical, then, is to be able to speak to one's own authority, to draw from one's experience and social location, and to interrogate a text within its context. To be critical is to explore work 'behind the scenes' and learn more than the content of media. To be critical is to not just know something, but to understand why and how it is known and to reflect on the process of learning. A teacher can point out racism in a text, for example, but until the student understands their own race embodiment, sees how race is represented in media both through content and the means of production, explores how race is discussed and treated in the broader society, and thinks through the permutations of race representation, they are not given the opportunity to fully enact critical thinking. If media education is to extend to action, young people will need to be able to create media that, for example, comments upon race in order to enact critical action. This process takes time, energy, and a willingness on the part of the teacher to 'let go' of the perceived correct answer.

A text may indeed be racist – and there are clearly countless examples – but until a student can come to that conclusion on their own, they are not practicing genuine critical thinking. The aim of media education, therefore, is to "enable [young people] to reflect systematically on the process of reading and writing [media], to understand and to analyse their own experience as readers and writers" (Buckingham, 2003, p. 141). Reflection and self-evaluation are crucial elements in the process of critical thinking because they enable one's internal knowledge to be made external within a community of learners (Buckingham, 2003). Critical thinking is *not* demystification (Masterman, 1985) where the teacher has access to all the 'correct' answers. Instead, it is an evolving process of co-created knowledge.

5   Technology in the Classroom

One major concern in the 21st century classroom is how to manage and make use of digital technology. Buckingham (2003) argues that media education is teaching *about*, not teaching *through*, the media, and yet classrooms and schools are under great pressure to utilize technology as teaching tools. Buckingham (2007) argues there is a confusion between using technology as a tool and teaching about technology as its own subject; he points out that "it's not the technology itself that makes the difference. At best, it is an enabler of other changes in teaching method" (p. 70). Overall, schools have difficulty keeping up with rapid changes in society and fall short with technology access and application. Simply *possessing* technology in a classroom is not helpful; the technology must be utilized efficiently and effectively. Buckingham (2007) further cautions that there must be clarity of purpose in using technology, that there is "fundamental confusion between the use of technology as a 'tool' for subject learning and technology as a separate subject in its own right" (p. 65). Tyner (1998) illustrates how the Clinton administration's push for computers in classrooms meant that while many classrooms had computers, teachers were provided with no mechanism for employing them. There is an underlying anxiety for teachers who do not integrate technology into their classrooms or lesson plans, an anxiety which may be because they are unclear about the value of technological inclusion (Buckingham, 2007).

Education scholars Long and Riegle (2002) and Darling-Hammond et al. (2005a) argue that technology comprehension is a necessary part of teachers' repertoires. Both teachers and teacher-educators must be able to make use of

CRITICAL MEDIA LITERACY

computers for their own knowledge as well as make use of them in the classroom (Long & Riegle). Students will need to make use of digital technology in future jobs, so schools must take on some responsibility to prepare students as part of their learning (Darling-Hammond et al., 2005a). Teachers must be involved in the process of technology inclusion and application. Otherwise, in a repeat of the 1990s, there will be classrooms filled with dust-generating gadgets.

Technology inclusion must be approached with caution. It is not uncommon for corporations to provide free technology to schools. After exiting his role as NYC Schools Chancellor, Joel Klein took a position with the technology branch of Rupert Murdoch's NewsCorp, tasked with developing a tablet specifically for school students (Otterman, 2016). Google announced in March 2018 that it would spend $300 million over three years to support quality journalism, funding various projects, to support middle and high school students to be smarter about their news and online information consumption (Stelter, 2018). In addition to providing schools with Microsoft technology, the corporation also opens and operates schools around the globe ("Microsoft schools program," n.d.). Since 2012, Verizon has given free technology, internet access, and hands-on learning experiences to under-resourced schools through their Verizon Innovative Learning program ("Building a brighter future for millions of kids," n.d.). While all these corporations may get much sought-after technologies into classrooms and facilitate learning, the technologies serve as surveillance of students, allowing the corporation to monitor all their activities while branding education. Access to young people's data is masked within corporate benevolence.

More well-known is the battle for school access between Apple and Google. Apple is one of many technology corporations seeking to infiltrate media education. Apple's efforts to provide iPads for classrooms are presented as corporate benevolence. The iPad is described as enhancing student and teacher creativity. The Apple website reads:

> [The iPad] enables endless opportunities to create hands-on, customizable learning experiences. Reach more students with apps and books geared to any level or subject. Develop your own interactive materials with iBooks Author. Organize and deliver your lessons with iTunes U. Discover a world of possibilities with iPad. ("Chromebook sales to families ...," n.d., apple.com)

Not to be outdone, the Google Chromebook presents itself as the responsible and most trusted technology for the classroom, and as flexible for both classroom and home use, with the enticing "access to the apps [students] know and love and long-life battery so students never have to stop learning" ("Chromebook sales to families ...," google.com).

What is not mentioned, of course, is that both Apple and Google will monitor everything accessed via the devices. Students, their families, and their schools are monitored and all their data is captured (Goodman, 2015; Pasquale, 2015). When individual families purchase Chromebooks, the company gives a percentage to the family's Parent Teacher Association (PTA). Here, corporate benevolence masks data mining; the school's PTA must enroll with Google to receive the discount code and families must use the code to buy the eligible Chromebook. Chromebook promotes itself as a better product than the iPad because it is considerably less expensive. The iPad is approximately $350 while, depending on the carrier brand, the Chromebook can cost under $200. Because the Chromebook is non-proprietary, it can be purchased on multiple devices, rather than tied specifically and exclusively to one platform, like Apple products. While cost is certainly something to consider, debates about price mask the reality of constant surveillance, specifically of minors, tacitly approved by parents and teacher who are not given 'opt out' options. Google partners with the National PTA (NPTA) to provide a digital citizenship course for children and related courses for parents. Google is supported by the NPTA, the Family Online Safety Institute, and the International Society for Technology in Education – three organization who are financially supported by Google. The lessons are branded with Google's name on every page, the color scheme and icons resemble Google's images, and the content focuses on how to traverse the internet more cautiously. The lessons do not question the role played by search engines, content providers, or social media platforms, all of whom monitor every single movement of users' online activity (Singer & Maheshwari, 2018).

The adoption of corporate content and tools comes at an ideological price for schools and students. To have access to the technology, one must accept the terms of service that include continuous monitoring. For schools and classrooms desperate for resources, it is an unfair choice: They provide their students with access to cutting-edge technologies for little to no out-of-pocket costs. In so doing, they sign away any modicum of privacy and put the control of resources into the hands of massively powerful corporations. In context, the benevolence of Google is less important to the corporation than their profit goals. Responding to the development of Project Dragonfly, a search tool that would capitulate to China's censorship model, over 300 Google employees signed an open letter critiquing the company for choosing profit over ethics (Salinas & D'Onfro, 2018).

What must be remembered is that while there may be advantages and disadvantages to technology inclusion, it is imperative to understand the

CRITICAL MEDIA LITERACY 29

application of technology in context. Technology inclusion must be recognized "in the light of other changes" (Buckingham, 2007, p. 91), including the political economy of children's culture, changes in policy, and social situations of young people's lives. Young people are empowered as consumers (even if their parent/guardian is paying the bills); even a cursory glance at the iPad and Chromebook websites reveals happy children working and playing together on the machines. What Buckingham (2007) cautions is that scenes such as these must be understood as the power of *consumption,* not necessarily the power of *citizenship.* Critical media literacy emphasizes developing sophisticated *citizens* not more adept *consumers* (Lewis & Jhally, 1998).

6   Conclusion: What's Missing?

There is a major gap in this chapter: *How* critical media literacy education gets into classrooms in a sustainable manner. In the United States, teachers and prospective teachers are not formally trained in media literacy as part of their teacher education. There are many unknowns in efforts to include media literacy in classrooms: If it is agreed upon that young people need media literacy in their schooling, how are teachers to weave it into their work? What resources and support do teachers need in order to be competent in their own media literacy knowledge as well as how to apply it? How can teachers of various subjects infuse media literacy as part of their curriculum?

First in 1990, and again in 2003, Buckingham pointed out there is no professional career track for teachers interested in being media literacy educators. The same statement can be made today: There is no established career track for media educators. In the majority of public schools, there is no job line for media literacy teachers and there is no particular professional development trajectory for teachers interested in media literacy. Teachers may add media literacy components to their classes, they may weave the study of media into their curriculum, but they will not be media literacy teachers. If interested in media literacy inclusion, they must do so on their own or make use of minimal available resources. If courses in media literacy can be added to teacher education, there may not be a clear career path for media literacy teachers, per se, but there will be the opportunity to integrate media literacy across subject matters.

The next two chapters discuss how prospective teachers are educated and the politics of the classroom space to make the argument that teacher training in critical media literacy is a needed next step in order to strengthen both teachers' skills and classroom work in media literacy.

CHAPTER 3

The Education of Training Teachers

Abstract

This chapter focuses on the role of teacher training, tracing its history as something largely ignored or deemed superfluous, to the apex of tension between multiple iterations of a neoliberal perspective on the purpose of schooling and the best way to prepare people to enact that purpose.

1 Introduction

> Sitting behind [Pa] on the board laid across the bobsled, Laura did not say anything, either. There was nothing to say. She was on her way to teach school.
>
> Only yesterday she was a schoolgirl; now she was a schoolteacher. This had happened so suddenly ... she did not really know how to do it. She had never taught school, and she was not sixteen years old yet. Even for fifteen, she was small; and now she felt very small. (Ingalls-Wilder, 1943, pp. 1–2)

So begins Chapter 1, "Laura leaves home" in *These happy golden years*, the eighth of the nine-book, fictionalized autobiographical "Little House" series, written by Laura Ingalls Wilder, focusing on her 19th century prairie upbringing. Laura's experience as a new teacher is one reflective of much of the history of teaching: She completed school at age 15 and was believed to possess enough knowledge to be at the front of a classroom (in a one-room schoolhouse with mixed-age children). She received no special training; she is single and teaching is a good job for young women, especially one who must help with the tuition for her blind sister's specialized college education. Later in the academic year, she will take a test to become a certified teacher, which will ideally give her better placement at a school closer to her home. At the end of the story, Laura leaves teaching when she gets married and needs to help work the family farm and raise her daughter.

Laura's fear and anticipation reveals a lot about the structure and organization of teacher training and teaching. Her story may be fictionalized and embedded in its 19th century context, but it reveals larger truths about the

© KONINKLIJKE BRILL NV, LEIDEN, 2020 | DOI: 10.1163/9789004416765_003

THE EDUCATION OF TRAINING TEACHERS   31

process of teaching. This chapter focuses on the role of teacher training, tracing its history as something largely ignored or deemed superfluous, to the apex of tension between multiple iterations of a neoliberal perspective on the purpose of schooling and the best way to prepare people to enact that purpose.

2   History of Teacher Education

Since the early days of classroom-based education in the United States, there have been debates over how best to prepare those interested in teaching. Teachers in the 17th and 18th centuries were an inconsistent group at best. Some prospective teachers were experts in their chosen subjects, possessing a formal education, while others could barely read or write.

Through much of the 19th century, it was believed there was no need to teach anyone how to teach. In Lucas' (1997) history of teacher education, he writes, "the notion that prospective school teachers need formal preparatory training for their work, apart from whatever regular academic studies they might have pursued would have attracted scant attention and even less popular support" (p. 3). Overall, teaching was considered supplemental work to one's full-time job and was entered on a part-time, temporary basis (Lucas). Those who took on classroom reaching were presumed to be available for only a limited time.

The commonly held belief through much of the 19th century was that anyone with familiarity of a subject could easily teach it (Labaree, 2008). Preposterous was the notion that teachers needed any special training. Teachers were expected to transmit commonly-agreed upon data to a collection of passive students, to manage the behavior of the students, and to follow direction from administrators (Hansen, 2008). Teachers were 'middle management,' a conduit of information from a perceived authority to perceived subordinates. What was unclear then and remains unclear today is how the administrative authorities came by their expertise. As will be shown in Chapter 4, those in charge of teachers, schools, and teacher education often have little to no experience in classrooms. This disjointed professional trajectory stunts any clear level of professional development in the field.

Increased democratization in education shifted the expectations for teacher readiness. Growing in the 19th century was the belief that more young people deserved formal, classroom-based education in order to participate fully in society (Lucas, 1997). In 1827, Massachusetts was the first state to make elementary education free to everyone (Lucas). Compulsory, no-cost, non-religious schools open to all members of a community increased in popularity, outweighing the argument that schooling should remain private (Lucas).

For a long time, 'public' schools remained institutions of elite families who could survive without their children's paid labor (Lueck, 2018). Young women, people of color, the poor, immigrants, the physically disabled, and those with cognitive learning challenges were offered less prestigious educations (if they were educated at all), but the public school did expand the possibilities for an increased quantity of young people. The common school, argued for by Horace Mann in the early 19th century, was:

> ... intended to provide a universal base of knowledge to be shared by all citizens, free of charge ... the public school would be the safeguard of the republic, which would benefit from the general education and enlightenment of the populace. (Lueck, 2018, theatlantic.com)

The high school grew out of the common school and was so called because of its elevated status; its purpose was to extend learning to a more advanced level (Lueck). A "simple but profound principle" was held steadfast for over a century, that "every child is entitled to an education that is free and accessible" (Cookson et al., 2018, p. 1).

By the early 20th century, more children in the United States were going to school than in any other nation (Long & Riegle, 2002). The increased democratization of education did not literally mean schooling for all, but it did create the foundation for free, compulsory education. There were approximately 10,000 graduates in the late 1860s, 100,000 at the start of the 20th century, and over 1 million by the 1930s (Lueck, 2018). Schools began to take on the appearance and organization of assembly lines: The division of grades based on age, grouped into elementary, junior, and high schools with set times devoted to specific subject matters per grade (Long & Riegle) all of which matched a factory model of organization and division of labor (or, in this case, learning). This model – roughly grades 1–6, 7–9, 10–12 – has changed minimally in the intervening years. Students were expected to comprehend the standards set forth at each grade and move forward with their cohort to the next grade. While it is true that more young people were educated than ever before, and while it was an effective model for many young people, there was very little room for variation in teaching or flexibility in learning. Schools were largely based in neighborhood communities with local control held by public officials (Labaree, 2008) and the training, certification, and hiring of teachers was largely a local matter (Lucas, 1997). Students were expected to receive the information provided with little to no contribution of their own design. The absence of innovation flavors much of the development of structured schooling and teacher preparation.

THE EDUCATION OF TRAINING TEACHERS   33

As public schooling grew in popularity and more children started attending school, it became clear that more teachers were needed. Drawing on the well-established belief that women were responsible for nurturing and care-giving, the 1800s saw the rise of the feminized teaching force (Lucas, 1997). While this was a boon for women's labor and increased their independence, it marked an early and lasting negation of the value of teaching. 'Nurturing' was not considered a key skill for any male-focused profession. While female teachers were willing and able to fill a need, they also worked for less pay than men (Labaree, 2008), effectively minimizing the seriousness attached to the profession.

The increase in young people attending school and the need for teachers to teach them fostered the need for a trained, professional teaching force. The normal school was believed to be the ideal, if controversial, teacher train-ing location (Lucas, 1997). From the outset, there was skepticism of normal schools' usefulness or purpose and the lingering belief that teachers did not need training, led to the question of "whether normal preparatory training sat-isfied any genuine need whatsoever" (Lucas, p. 29). The normal school was the location where women, specifically, could get an advanced education. At the time, this rendered teaching automatically less important while, simultane-ously, because of its route to intellectual achievement and financial indepen-dence, made it very important to women. As normal schools began shifting and higher education enrollments increased, the gender divide in teaching became more obvious. More men were entering higher education, leaving more space – but less viability – for women at normal schools (Labaree, 2008). One major concern with normal schools was their specificity; graduating with a teaching degree enabled only one career option, which served to limit enroll-ment and retention. Those seeking advanced degrees wanted greater flexi-bility. Simultaneously, changes in American society, especially urbanization, industrialization, and post-World War I global responsibilities demanded a more educated workforce and therefore, a more consistently trained teacher (Long & Riegle, 2002).

Teacher education could no longer afford to be so specialized as the normal school offered but could not maintain financial solvency with such a particular offering, so normal schools, by and large, became absorbed into colleges and universities (Long & Riegle, 2002; Lucas, 1997). Education schools and teacher training programs took on the ethos of the universities of which they were a part and because of the particular focus within the larger university, teacher education became a "cash cow'" with relatively loose standards and expec-tations, where the education school could "generate a nice profit for the rest of the university" (Labaree, 2008, p. 300). Teaching colleges, and ultimately colleges and universities with education and teacher education programs, could provide greater flexibility for students and more stability within programs. Whether this was the best model for teacher preparation remained contested, however teacher education programs within universities has been the model, relatively unchanged, since the early 20th century (Labaree).

Since teacher training has been established, there have been complaints about it. The development of formal, codified teacher training did little to shift the perception of the professionalization of the field. According to Darling-Hammond (2006), the complaints have circled around "perceptions of program fragmentations, weak content, poor pedagogy, disconnection from schools, and inconsistent oversight of teachers-in-training" (p. 6). These complaints are shared with the persistent belief that "teachers are basically technicians serving the interests of those with economic and political power" (Hansen, 2008, p. 10). "Basic reading, writing, and arithmetic skills and a disposition to work hard and conscientiously" was all that was perceived necessary for a complete education (Long & Riegle, 2002, p. xi). If the K-12 school organization took on the flavor of the assembly line, so too did teacher education.

The structure and organization of teacher education shifted slightly in the late 20th century, adopting the neoliberal ideology of the free market. Private companies cropped up to provide rapid, efficient routes to classrooms and many states accepted alternative routes to teacher certification. These routes were generally quicker to complete, with fewer standards, less training for prospective teachers, and more avenues through the bureaucracy of private, state, and federal policies and expectations (Cornbleth, 2014; Darling-Hammond, 2006). They often promise prospective teachers a cutting-edge experience that will make them invaluable in schools (Blanchard, 2013; Jackson, 2016) but the flashy marketing and savvy language often leave participants adrift (DiMartino & Butler-Jesson, 2018). How to most thoroughly prepare potential teachers for classroom work remains a topic of debate.

The free market approach to education often means that those with little actual experience in education direct educational change. Solomon's (2002) analysis of the Edison Schools, a private, education-for-profit corporation, highlights this. H. Christopher Whittle, the founder of Edison Schools, has no educational background. He was an entrepreneur who attempted to build a media empire, including Channel 1, the news program designed for classrooms where students are compelled to watch advertising. Whittle took on too many commercial ventures and his budding empire collapsed. He started the Edison Schools in 1992 as a way to focus on one, single enterprise and hired two educational professionals who argued in favor of free market principles. According to Solomon, "Edison seeks to turn the management of public and charter

THE EDUCATION OF TRAINING TEACHERS   35

schools into a profit making enterprise," yet in its first 10 years, Edison did not earn a profit and "sustained net operating losses in every fiscal quarter since it began operations" (p. 1297). Edison seeks to decrease expenses through limitation on education specialists, including special education teachers, employing part-time teachers, those with less experience or, if possible, those who are uncertified.

3   Teacher Education Debate

The overarching debate concerning the need for comprehensive teacher education is framed as a choice between academic ability and subject matter knowledge or pedagogical preparation. Arguing that pedagogical preparation is a key part of teacher education, Darling-Hammond (2006) writes, "What looks easy from the students' vantage point – giving gripping lectures, holding scintillating discussions, assigning challenging tasks, providing insightful feedback – is a function of behind-the-scenes planning, resting on many bodies of knowledge about learning, curriculum, and teaching" (p. 30). Darling-Hammond, Holtzman, Gatlin, and Vasquez-Heilig (2005b) argue in favor of teaching potential teachers about curriculum and curriculum development. While Darling-Hammond and colleagues provide a comprehensive defense of university-based teacher training that provides prospective teachers with thorough preparation in both theory and practice, they do so in an environment driven by market forces and follow its ethos of hyper individuality and competition. They offer a better model for teacher training than non-university-based approaches, but one that still supports a 'one-size-fits-all' model of schooling.

The ethos of teaching is a conflicted topic in the United States. K-12 and higher education teaching is observed in multiple, draining ways. Mehta (2013) critiques the American approach to teacher education, writing "there is no widely agreed-upon knowledge base, training is brief or non-existent, the criteria for passing licensing exams are much lower than in other fields, and there is little professional guidance" (nytimes.com). University-based teacher education programs are blamed for preferring a scientific, versus a humanist, approach to teacher training, one that relies on research and evaluation rather than human engagement and interaction (Sockett, 2001). In her meditations on teaching and learning, hooks (2003, 2010) reimagines how to approach the act of teaching. She observes that teaching – from early childhood education through university teaching – can be exhausting because "the classroom is one of the most dynamic work settings precisely because we are given such a short amount of time to do so much" (2003, p. 14). At expensive colleges and universities, "there is an even greater tendency to see professors as workers who have less status than students, since the students see themselves (via their parents) as paying the wages of their teachers" (2010, p. 112). While it is largely not true that tuition fees pay faculty salaries, in a nation so conflicted over the value of education and teaching, it is easy to understand how this myth develops. There is little agreement if teachers are professionals or vocational tradespeople, are meant to lift the prospects of students, or serve their needs, are operating under scientific, or humanist, theories.

Unfortunately, the humanist approach may serve to weaken the argument in favor of formal teacher education because it runs the risk of relying on the assumption that teaching is an intuitive act. Darling-Hammond (2006) paints intuitive teaching as a scenario where "someone knows something and then 'teaches' it to others" constructing a "fairly straightforward transmission model" (p. 8). Darling-Hammond (2006) argues vociferously against the notion of teaching as an intuitive or transmissive act, noting that effective teachers "link what students already know and understand to new information, correcting misimpressions, guiding learners' understanding through a variety of activities, providing opportunities for application of knowledge, giving useful feedback that shapes performance, and individualizing for students' distinctive learning needs" (p. 8). In other words, teaching is dynamic and relies on vast knowledge and management skills.

The debates about the value and effectiveness around teacher education include concerns about finances (Long & Riegle, 2002), questions of effectiveness and efficiency (Darling-Hammond, 2010), inconsistent training and absence of standards (Darling-Hammond, 2010), what matters for teacher education (Robertson, 2008), and how to keep pace with technological and social changes (Long & Riegle, 2002). Darling-Hammond (2006) believes the narratives about ineffective teacher training are poorly informed and should not be the guiding voice that informs policy decisions or investment in teacher preparation. Darling-Hammond (2006) argues that the kind of teacher training matters and even well-trained teachers may "feel unprepared for the real challenges they face in their work" (p. 34). The humanist element of teaching is often looked over as somehow less important.

In the United States, there are two main avenues for teacher education: College/university-based education schools and independent, alternative programs. Within these two main avenues, there are multiple types of teacher education and no two programs are the same. Individual instructors and students bring their own subjectivity and individual schools and programs have their own foci. The following discussion looks at the 'big picture' differences between styles/intents of programs and how they represent the field of teacher

THE EDUCATION OF TRAINING TEACHERS 37

education. It is *not* an exhaustive discussion of all the teacher education programs in the United States, but rather, a sample of styles that illustrate the broad divisions and similarities.

4 Arguing with Alternative Teacher Education

The arguments against traditional, university-based teacher education rely on a free-market approach, favoring speed and competition. They extend Friedman's (1955) argument against government (public) schools in favor of charter schools and voucher programs, under the argument that increased competition strengthens the market and translates directly to increased quality. By extension, "in line with free-market ideology, this system follows the logic of the survival of the fittest: 'failing' schools, like failing companies, will either be publicly shamed into improving themselves, or simply cease to exist at all" (Buckingham, 2011, p. 214). It was Friedman's goal that public schools would, in fact, cease to exist.

Alternative programs favor easier access to classrooms, with less preparation for prospective teachers and fewer protections for classroom teachers, with greater power located at district levels (Darling-Hammond & Rothman, 2015). This runs the risk of more unprepared teachers struggling in classrooms where the potential for being fired is a regular threat. Arguments against teacher education rest on the belief that the act of teaching does not require specialized skills or knowledge and that anything that needs to be learned about the act of teaching can be learned on-site, in the classroom, in real time (Darling-Hammond, 2006; Darling-Hammond & Rothman, 2015). Certainly, a struggle with on-site learning is that students are the receiving end of the teachers' learning curve and their education may be unduly effected.

In some cases, teacher certification is considered an obstacle to entry to the field. State-required certifications can be earned along the way, while already teaching in classrooms. Removing the lengthy training and education process undoubtedly gets more people into teaching and into classrooms more quickly, however, this happens at the expense of teacher salary and quality working conditions (Darling Hammond & Rothman, 2015). Alternatively trained teachers without state-certifications (those on emergency certifications or in progress) may not have union protection and may earn significantly lower salaries than certified teachers. Alternative teacher education programs are often highlighted for their efficiency and anti-bureaucratic approach. A leading conservative voice against university-based teacher education, The Thomas B. Fordham Foundation (1999), argues "outstanding candidates are often discouraged by the hurdles that the regulatory strategy loves to erect" (p. 7). Certification requirements are "burdensome" and those interested in teaching "are put off by the cost, in time and money, of completing a conventional preparation program" (p. 7). According to Chester E. Finn, Jr., the President of the Fordham Foundation (1999), a common-sense approach to teacher training includes eliminating all but the most needed regulations, locating personnel decisions at individual schools, and then holding schools accountable for student success. This echoes the assembly-line model of school organization: The pieces – teaching and learning – are meant to fit together, as designed, and if they do not, it is an individual flaw, not a design (structural) flaw.

When teachers and schools are run by private corporations, teachers and schools are inadvertently held accountable to corporate and private funders, not to communities and students (Cornbleth, 2014). Private corporations are not always as streamlined as they may present themselves. The Fordham Foundation, for example, funnels funding through the National Council on Teacher Quality (NCTQ), which, through a series of financial debacles whose discussion is beyond the scope of this text, can only accept private donations (Cornbleth). The Fordham Foundation (1999) believes potential teachers should be tested "for their knowledge and skills," principals should hire the teachers they need, and the focus of school quality should be on results as an assessment of what students are learning (p. 2). While this sounds enticing, there are no clearly defined standards for student learning (Ravitch, 2010), so any assessment of learning via this model is incomplete. This effectively eliminates any chance at success for those teachers working with struggling students or any options for struggling students to experience non-formulaic teaching. It is clear that an underlying motivation of these conservative voices is to eliminate educational support and stem the tide of democratized education.

While one might assume that training to be a teacher would include work in classrooms, some alternative teacher training programs do not have any in-classroom training components. Darling-Hammond and Rothman (2015) argue against these alternative programs because those without student teaching or preservice training "appear to have the least productive outcomes for their recruits and the students they teach" (p. 14). Studies have shown that by the third year of teaching, when alternatively-trained teachers have completed state certification requirements, there are few significant differences between teachers traditionally or alternatively trained. How these data are interpreted matters (Darling-Hammond & Rothman, 2015). Because of high attrition rates in the first years of teaching, it is unclear if third-year effectiveness is because lower performing teachers quit or because the teachers who remain seek out opportunities for additional training.

THE EDUCATION OF TRAINING TEACHERS
39

Furthermore, if teachers are doing their foundational learning 'on the job,' there are classrooms of young people who, through no fault of their own, receive a weaker education. In her continued critique of alternative programs, Darling-Hammond (1999/2008) argues alternative programs leave "teachers seriously underprepared" and are "significantly less effective" at preparing potential teachers than traditional university programs (p. 333). In these examples of concern – 'least productive outcomes,' differences in approaches to teaching, and 'significantly less effective' – the measurements are often hard to quantify precisely. A major concern with the alternative programs is that they leave potential teachers without a variety of needed skills, including skills for how to adapt to shifting classroom scenarios. Alternatively-trained teachers are not taught the skills needed to maneuver a dynamic classroom, leaving students less educated and resulting in teachers leaving the profession at higher than average rates (Darling-Hammond, 1999/2008).

Alternative programs present the process of becoming a teacher as an exciting adventure, one easily interpreted as middle-class benevolence for poor children. The argument against traditional teacher education uses 'natural' and 'intuitive' teacher skills as a smokescreen to distract from their reliance on market principles that pull education out of the public sphere and into private, for profit, corporations. For example, Rhee and Oakley's (2008) Practitioner Teacher Program worked with alternative teacher training programs to "aggressively recruit career changers to make the switch into education" (p. 373). The Practitioner Teacher Program, launched in 2002, helped states license prospective teachers in roughly a six-eight week period. Training happened over the summer, in the hiring district where the teacher would eventually work, so the trainees could get experience with the students with whom they would most likely work. Echoing the ethos of hyper individuality and the promise of the market, Rhee and Oakley (2008) write:

> We inculcate the teachers with the belief that they, personally, are responsible for ensuring the achievement of every child in their classroom, no matter the external influences at play. We train teachers that understanding the whole child, including community/environment/home life, is a crucial aspect in order to see the child reach his or her fullest academic potential, but we send and reinforce the explicit message that the teacher still has personal responsibilities for the outcomes that are achieved in his or her classroom. (p. 374)

Is it reasonable to ask one teacher to be wholly responsible for a child's achievement, irrespective of any outside influence? While it is admirable to understand the whole child, can the skills needed to do this be learned in a six-eight week time period? Indeed, it may be more accurate – but certainly less flashy – to note that understanding the whole child is a continuous, ever-evolving process over the course of one's career. This approach presumes that the recruited business experts' skills are easily transferrable to the classroom. If a person decides after time in one profession that they want the challenge of a different profession, they may not be able to ease into it with limited training. If a business executive, for example, decides to pursue a career in medicine, medical school requirements will not be waived just because the person has good ideas, is motivated, and can bring certain skills to the position. The Practitioner Teacher Program partnered with states to secure teaching licenses, effectively eliminating the public work of the state. This echoes Buckingham's (2011) observation:

> In education as in many other areas, the state is moving away from being a provider of public services to being a commissioner or contractor, or a 'partner' with the private sector, while the private sector is widely believed to have superior expertise in terms of innovation, management and efficiency. (pp. 212–213)

Prior to her work in alternative teacher training, Rhee was most well known as the Chancellor of the Washington, D.C. public schools where she worked to effectively eliminate public schools in favor of charter schools and voucher programs. Her work did not improve the Washington, D.C. school system by any measurable capacity (Brown, Strauss, & Stein, 2018). Furthermore, while making teachers "personally responsible" for student success sounds bold, it is a dangerous precedent that envisions teachers as alone in their quest, isolated from colleagues or collaborative opportunities. If teachers are responsible "no matter the external influences at play," then not only the teacher but the classroom and the student are isolated as well. Students, teachers, classrooms, and schools operate in a complex context where external factors, both implicit and explicit, must be considered. Implicitly, the assumption of public schools as operating under business principles cannot be ignored. Explicitly, systemic racism, sexism, and classism must be addressed.

Teachers that are trained business people will run schools like businesses, embracing a corporate ethos that effectively eliminates any local, state, or federal oversight, eventually realizing Friedman's (1955) dream to remove the government from schooling. Public school in the vision of private enterprise is no longer public. Targeting business professionals, Rhee and Oakley (2008) shift the paradigm of the new teacher from one who prepares, in college and/or

THE EDUCATION OF TRAINING TEACHERS 41

graduate school, for a teaching career, to one taking on teaching as a fun career change. This is not to argue that one must know, at age 18, that teaching is a desired career path. My concern is that the image constructed is one that views teaching as a side project, something to tackle after the real (private sector) work is completed. This further de-professionalizes teaching by reinforcing it as a second choice, after more lucrative work has been realized.

The recruitment of business professionals also shifts the paradigm of teaching and learning to a more corporate model. Mid-career professionals interested in teaching may have some degree of business acumen and/or professional skills assumed easily transferrable to the classroom. Rhee and Oakley (2008) write that their Fellows found that education schools did not account for their work as professionals, acknowledge their content knowledge or work experience, or their need to balance full-time work with teacher preparation training. That is, traditional teacher training programs do not prioritize business acumen as valid teaching preparation. The alternative program run by Rhee and Oakley rewarded those professionals who make career changes to teaching by fast tracking them through the process of preparation. Systems set in place to protect quality of teacher preparation are re-imagined as burdensome and restrictive for those with professional skills (and, conceivably, professional degrees) who want to shift gears to teaching.

When conservative alternative training organizations and foundations use the language "accountable by the marketplace," "deregulated," "skills-based accountability," and "sanctions" (Fordham Foundation, 1999, p. 8) they re-imagine schools as businesses in the private interest. The state's only responsibilities should be administrative, assuring that prospective teachers know their subjects – as proven through a test – and have no "record of misbehavior" (Fordham Foundation, p. 11). A term such as "regulation," effectively meaning protection and oversight of quality, is rendered as wholly negative and overly bureaucratic.

Popular alternative or supplemental teacher education programs rely on the appeal of efficiency and speed while they work to undermine teachers' unions and displace veteran teachers. One of the most popular alternative teacher training programs in the United States is Teach for America (TFA). TFA recruits high-achieving recent graduates from competitive colleges and places them in high-needs urban and rural schools ("Teach for America," n.d., teachforamerica.org). TFA is often held as evidence for the lack of need for lengthy, formal teacher training (Darling-Hammond, 2006). TFA recruits are trained over the summer, commit to two years of teaching, and are then given emergency licenses to begin teaching in the fall (Darling-Hammond et al., 2005b). According to their research, Darling-Hammond et al. (2005b) "find no instance where uncertified Teach for America teachers performed as well as standard certified teachers of comparable experience levels teaching in similar settings" (p. 20). According to data analyzed, students taught by uncertified TFA fellows were found to be two weeks to three months behind students taught by certified teachers. Students at the highest-needs schools lost one-two years of progress between K-6th grade when taught by uncertified teachers. When TFA fellows achieved certification – and the training that happens during the certification process – they performed similarly to traditionally trained and certified teachers.

According to former TFA fellows (Blanchard, 2013; Jackson, 2016), the actual experience of training does not match TFA's stated intent. Gary Rubenstein, a TFA fellow from its first class, argues that TFA fellows and administrators engage in 'teacher bashing' and undermine unions and traditional support systems (Jackson, 2016). Olivia Blanchard, a TFA fellow starting in 2011, was led to believe that it was her responsibility, as a TFA recruit, to close the achievement gap, a challenge that, she was told, was not being met by out-of-touch veteran teachers. This emphasis on competition and individual prowess echoes the logic of neoliberalism and makes public schools complicit in market logic. More pertinent for Blanchard and her colleagues, it fostered resentment between the TFA fellows and traditionally educated teachers. Blanchard's five weeks of teaching practice was with a small group of nine students taking summer school classes to pass a reading exam needed to move to the 4th grade; this practice in no way prepared her for the 30-student, 5th grade classroom where she taught math and science. She counters TFA's claims that they offer 10 hours per week of classroom practice with her two 90-minute classes per week and challenges the claim they provide 'experienced teachers' for support, which, for her, translated to a TFA alumnus with about two years classroom experience.

In their precise critique of the marketing of education, DiMartino and Butler-Jessen (2018) detail the recruitment process of TFA. As a "consumer based organization," TFA seeks to expand its roster of teacher candidates "via marketing, in the form of recruiting" (p. 104). TFA plasters campuses with advertising materials in a widespread and strategic manner, contacting students beyond those who expressed interest, and making it clear that an education background is not necessary. For high-achieving college students under pressure to secure a job, it is hard to fight the enticement of near-guaranteed employment upon graduation.

While TFA recruits are generally strong students, they are not well-prepared to be teachers, especially in high risk, low-performing schools. In a review of the NYC school system, Nazaryan (2016) observes TFA's decreased popularity, the shortcomings of other alternative programs, and the lack of appreciable

THE EDUCATION OF TRAINING TEACHERS   43

difference from Facebook founder Mark Zuckerberg's $100 million influx of cash to the Newark, New Jersey public school system, all of which might lend more credence to more traditional types of reform. Though traditional education reform has been framed as old-fashioned, out of touch, and overly reliant on teachers' unions, there is no compelling evidence that the alternative programs are producing better teachers who, in turn, produce more successful students.

5   Arguing with Traditional Teacher Education

Despite appeals for efficiency and claims for more precise and relevant training, university-based teacher education remains the more effective model for long-term, sustained teacher preparation. While traditional, university-based teacher training is not flawless and needs revision and updating, it is, at its foundation, the most responsible way to train prospective teachers and the best option for their future students. Traditional teacher education programs have been criticized for being slow to respond to change, lengthy in prep time, and expensive to pursue (Darling-Hammond, 1999/2008). Despite these critiques, traditional teacher education deserves to be remedied, not deleted. Teacher education takes on the flavor and interest of its home institution. This means education schools are susceptible to multiple pressures, including any changes in state regulations or accreditation expectations, the shifting priorities of the university, the labor market of their communities, and of course, the pressures associated with re-branding teacher education in the corporate image (Cornbleth, 2014). Education schools appear sluggish and old-fashioned compared to a six-week training program with promised employment. However, rapid-fire teacher training, with minimal time to process the learning, results in a just-in-time mentality for teachers and teaching.

A university that takes the education of future teachers seriously will produce stronger, more adaptable teachers. To take teacher education and preparation seriously is to support and foster the professionalization of teachers. Darling-Hammond (2010) argues that counterproductive conditions that belittle both teacher preparation and teaching:

> will continue until teaching becomes a profession like medicine, architecture, accounting, engineering, or law, in which every practitioner has the opportunity and the expectations to master the knowledge and skills needed for effective practice, and makes the moral commitment to use this knowledge in the best decisions of their clients. (p. 196)

Mehta (2013) extends the metaphor of professionalization, writing:

> Teaching requires a professional model, like we have in medicine, law, engineering, accounting, architecture, and many other fields. In these professions, consistency of quality is created less by holding individual practitioners accountable and more by building a body of knowledge, carefully training people in that knowledge, requiring them to show expertise before they become licensed, and then using their professions' standards to guide their work. (nytimes.com)

To become akin to these highly specialized professions is to both respect the education of teachers and recognize that while there might be some with a natural aptitude for teaching, all prospective teachers deserve comprehensive in-depth education in theory and practice. Furthermore, all students, regardless of economic class, geography, or race, deserve well-educated teachers.

Teacher education programs are significantly different from each other. The one consistent thing that can be said about teacher training is there is no consistency. The United States has over 1400 teacher education programs which are regulated differently across the 50 states (Darling-Hammond & Rothman, 2015). There are approximately 13,600 school districts across the United States (Back to School Statistics, n.d.) that operate with minimal federal oversight (Long & Riegle, 2002). In-class student teaching time ranges from five to 30 weeks and may or may not be in a school that partners with a university-based teacher training program (Darling-Hammond & Rothman, 2015). University-based teacher education programs tend to run longer in both coursework and student teaching than alternative programs and some alternative programs have no connections or relationships with colleges or universities (Long & Riegle, 2002). New teachers begin with a provisional license that lasts two-three years, in which time they must demonstrate proficiency and satisfactory performance in order to achieve a full license (Darling-Hammond & Rothman, 2015). The Thomas B. Fordham Foundation (1999) believes that even a two-year commitment to classroom-focused training is cumbersome and serves as an obstacle to potential teachers. Darling-Hammond (2006) counters that inadequate preparation "increased teacher attrition, which exacerbates the revolving door that contributes to teacher shortages" (p. 14).

In her prolific and consistent defense of traditional, university-based teacher education, Darling-Hammond (1999/2008, 2010, 2011) argues that prospective teachers deserve three to four years of training, including coursework and classroom practice, regular mentoring and professional development opportunities, plus competitive salaries. Well-trained teachers are more effective with students than alternatively trained teachers (Darling-Hammond, 1999/2008). Prospective teachers deserve to be trained in ways that support and encourage learning- and learner-centered approaches (Darling-Hammond, 2006). The learning-centered approach is "supportive of focused, in-depth learning that results in powerful thinking and proficient performance on the part of students" while the learner-centered portion is "responsive to individual students' experiences, interests, talents, needs, and cultural backgrounds (pp. 7–8). Learning how to build and adapt curriculum that represents and responds to students' lives, connects students with their learning, and supports equity is essential (Darling-Hammond et al., 2005a). Careful, attentive training can help teachers recognize their own privilege (Keiser, 2005), connecting them more authentically to their students.

The preparation and readiness of teachers is not found just in their preservice training but also in the opportunities for continued professional development. In the United States, salary incentives are often the motivation for professional development and quality opportunities are uneven, at best (Darling-Hammond & Rothman, 2015). Unfortunately, even when professional development opportunities are available, they are often "one-shot workshops" which are inconsistent in availability and shallow in their offerings (Darling-Hammond & Rothman, p. 19). To matter and to have a positive impact, professional development opportunities need to be more sustained, which "may explain why relatively few U.S. teachers say that the professional development they have experienced has impacted their practice" (Darling-Hammond & Rothman, p. 20). Because most education decisions are made at the state level, there are variations in what is available across the nation. States vary (greatly) in funding for pre-service and in-service education, in the standards of professional development opportunities, the relevancy for various teachers and professional staff, and the level of or commitment to requiring professional development (Darling-Hammond, 2000).

6   Commonalities between Approaches

What the alternative and traditional teacher training programs have in common in their current iterations is a 'one-sized-fits-all' perspective that bows to the pressures (and perceived rewards) of the market. Though she is a staunch defender of teacher education, Darling-Hammond and colleagues appear primed to accept and support an increase in charter schools, which effectively dismantles teachers' unions, and neighborhood schooling. In their analysis of the current face of education reform, Cookson et al. (2018) dissect the meanings and exaction of 'choice.' They note that 'choice' "has raised questions about the nature of the social contract to provide education to all children and about the efficacy of markets to provide good schools for all" (p. 1). Charter school management has connected the notion of 'choice' with automatically better schooling, which Cookson et al. (2018) are quick to point out is not always true. Despite ostensibly being public schools, many charter schools perform less effectively than the neighborhood public schools. Charter schools are known to increase segregation, admit fewer students with special needs, and choose among the highest performing students (Cookson et al., 2018).

Normalizing 'choice' as something that *is* a choice is risky. Giving 'choice' credence in the face of evidence against its veracity is dangerous. 'Choice' is generally a term adopted by non-profit and for-profit businesses as a mechanism to increase charter schools and vouchers in order to decrease public schools and dismantle teachers' unions (Strauss, 2014; Burris & Ravitch, 2018). While they critique 'choice,' Cookson et al. (2018) do so in a way that opens the possibility for compromise through fixing the concrete availability of actual choice rather than seeing choice as a tool of the market designed to undo the work of public institutions. A particular concern with Cookson et al.'s approach is their negligence of school governance. In an op-ed piece opposing their data interpretation, Burris and Ravitch (2018) write, "we know from experience that charter schools and vouchers drain finances and the students they want from the district public schools, causing budget cuts, teacher layoffs and larger class sizes in the schools that enroll the most children" (washingtonpost.com). Both 'choice' and alternative teacher education are very real things whose emphasis on personal preference and efficiency mask their dismantling of public institutions.

The alternative, fast-track training programs may be more obvious in their desire to re-shape schools in a business model while making less room for collaboration or community engagement and, often, effectively removing impoverished youth of color or those with special learning needs from the normative classroom space. The traditional, university-based models struggle as well. In its relatively unchanged state, traditional teacher education lags behind creative, innovative change making and structures both teaching and learning in a skills-based, check-box set of accomplishments. Both models appear disinterested in or unable to address different learning needs or make sustainable inroads to shifting the larger opportunity gaps.

This is not to argue that high-needs schools should be left to their own devices or ignored in their plight to get committed teachers into their classrooms. Rather than plucking high-achieving, but underprepared, college graduates to work in communities dramatically different from their own, or

THE EDUCATION OF TRAINING TEACHERS   47

recruiting mid-career professionals with the opportunity to do something dramatically different in communities different from their own, a more holistic approach might be to work *within* communities, strengthening what is already there. To better serve economically struggling urban youth of color, prospective teachers of color may seek out teacher education programs with social justice-based curricula in order to receive better training for various populations (Achinstein & Ogawa, 2011). Supplemental programs, such as Grow Your Own (GYO), based out of Chicago, Illinois, work to support marginalized communities by forging relations between education schools, community organizations, and public schools to bring teachers of color to the classroom (Skinner & Schultz, 2011). Using critical pedagogy and critical race theory to inform their work, GYO's mission is to "improve teaching and learning in high-needs schools by recruiting and preparing community-based teachers and returning them to their local schools" (Schultz, Gillette, & Hill, 2011, p. 5).

Challenging the belief that well-educated or well-credentialed, but minimally trained, young people from outside the community can remedy schools, GYO creates partnerships *within* communities by recruiting those already working in schools, alumni, and community members to become educators under the belief that those invested in the community will be invested in *remedying* the community and that community collaboration "can prompt not only reflection, but also the potential to transform teacher education" (Schultz et al., 2011, pp. 5–6). With its emphasis on community, responsive techniques, and understanding of a variety of needs, this collaborative work stems the tide of neoliberalism.

Mehta (2013) argues that *how* teachers are trained matters less than attention paid to the quality of the school and the support teachers receive. The manner of training is less important than the attention paid to the efficacy of a particular school. Successful schools have "a clear mission, talented teachers, time for teachers to work together, longer school days or after-school programs, feedback cycles that lead to continuing improvements" (Mehta, 2013, nytimes.com). He sees the difference in quality between graduates of alternative and traditional programs to be "negligible." Looking at data from a ten-year period, between 1995–2004 in North Carolina, Clotfelter, Ladd, and Vigdor (2007) found that teachers with more formal credentials had a greater positive impact on student math learning, but minimal positive impact on reading achievement. Teacher training and professional development could not offset the negative effects of poverty (Clotfelter et al.). What might matter more is that well-trained teachers stay in teaching for longer, offering a degree of stability strugglings students might otherwise not experience. A significant concern is that the long-term value of in-depth teacher education is pushed aside for the quick hiring of less qualified teachers (Darling-Hammond, 2000).

On top of significant theoretical and practical training, the ideal is also to learn and practice more nuanced, in-depth practice. Hansen (2008) writes:

> Among the most prominent values influencing the scope and structure of teacher education programs today are preparation for work and life, academic learning, human development, and social justice, with the latter cast in some cases as respect for cultural diversity or multicultural education, and in others as civic or democratic education. (p. 12)

Keiser (2005) calls for social justice teacher education that not only prepares young people for the work force but also acknowledges their ability to make change in their communities. Teachers and schools "need to account for students' holistic well-being, as well as their test scores, and need to define school success by affective engagement, democratic participation, and citizenship, as well as by basic reading and math skills" (Keiser, 2005, pp. 32–33). In impoverished public schools in Baltimore, Maryland, Gillen (2014) works to construct a radical shift in class dynamics through involving young people in their own educational revolution. He calls for radical teachers to support student insurgency so that those on the fringes are more clearly seen and less easily dismissed. Unfortunately, despite massive transformations across all areas of society, teacher education and policy influence "have changed remarkably little in the past fifty or more years" (Long & Riegle, 2002, p. xvi).

Nuanced, in-depth practice cannot happen in rapid, alternative training or through a transmission model. Critical pedagogy scholar Freire (1970) argued against the transmission model in favor of a dialogic model where students and teachers work together. He writes that radical educators' efforts "must coincide with those of the students to engage in critical thinking and the quest for mutual humanization ... [teachers] must be partners of the students in their relations with them" (p. 75). Educators and students work together to co-create knowledge. hooks (2003) writes that "commitment to teaching well is a commitment to service" (p. 83), an increasingly difficult task in capitalist patriarchy. Kohl (2002) notes that teachers are listened to more often, and possibly in different ways, than they may initially think. He writes:

> Students interpret, reflect, analyze, and respond to the nuances of language in the classroom, and since most of the permitted language in the classroom is teacher talks, it is to that language that an excessive amount of student emotion and intelligence is committed. (p. 150)

Delpit (2002) notes that the culturally non-responsive classroom ignores students who do not 'fit' the standard expectation, writing, "when instruction is

THE EDUCATION OF TRAINING TEACHERS 49

stripped of children's cultural legacies, then they are forced to believe that the world and all the good things in it were created by others" (p. 41). Responsive pedagogy reaches students by connecting their lives to their learning, bridging their interests with academic requirements (Delpit).

7 Conclusion

In Mehta's (2016) summation of the radical suggestions laid out to reform education, he argues that despite generations of effort, little has changed at the core of education. The bureaucratic system of schooling, which made a certain sense in the 19th century as a way to standardize and organize education, is too cumbersome today. Teachers in this system do not have the necessary expertise and the 'one-size-fits-all' system of schooling is incapable of addressing individual need.

Traditional education schools are fundamentally more responsible in their training of prospective teachers, even as they are slow to respond to change and are often old-fashioned in their approach. Their fundamental effort is sound: Foster well-informed, well-rounded, deeply supported teachers. Prospective teachers deserve education in both theory and practice; they deserve the time to both learn and process their learning, then put their learning to practice in a carefully guided and supported way. They deserve to put that practice back to theory and interrogate their successes and struggles. Teacher education needs to be more flexible and more adaptable – to make it so does not mean the entire system needs to be upended. A particular tweak to the process of teacher training may result in profound positive change: The inclusion of critical media literacy learning as part of teachers' own classroom preparation. The next two chapters will outline and frame the space for the inclusion of critical media literacy through a discussion of the politics of the classroom (Chapter 4) and an exploration of critical media literacy's benefits (Chapter 5).

CHAPTER 4

Politicizing the Classroom

Abstract

This chapter examines the larger context of schooling and the politics of education. Through an exploration of reform, teacher, classroom, and student roles, this chapter explores the current environment of schooling.

1 Introduction

> Despite years of putting up with underperforming teachers, overcrowded classrooms, and a gradually deteriorating educational experience, American students reluctantly announced Tuesday that they would be giving the nation's public school system yet another chance this fall ... Admittedly they were a little reluctant to put their faith in the same flawed bureaucracy that, for decades now, has failed to close the ever-widening achievement gap and cannot fix painfully apparent budget inadequacies, the nation's K through 12 pupils told reporters that what eventually sealed their decision to return to school was a deep, unshakeable faith that the richest, most powerful country in the world would be able to meet the highest global standards for education. (*The Onion*, 2011)

The Onion, a satirical online newspaper, often comments on current events and their 'back-to-school' themed article is no exception. Humor can speak volumes as this 'article' does in its address of the structure of K-12 public schooling in the United States. The humor here is decidedly dark: Students are reluctant to return to school because of the obvious failings of their classrooms. Echoing Buckingham's (1990, 2007) argument that young people often come to their classrooms knowing more than for which they are given credit, the fictional children in the above 'article' are acutely aware of their schools' failings, but give them yet another chance. In satire there is truth: The achievement gap has not shrunk, budget choices do not appear to have any sustainable positive benefit, many schools struggle with too few resources, and yet, American schooling remains in extraordinarily high regard.

Using satire as an entry point, this chapter builds on the debates of teacher training to examine the larger context of schooling and the politics of

© KONINKLIJKE BRILL NV, LEIDEN, 2020 | DOI: 10.1163/9789004416765_004

POLITICIZING THE CLASSROOM   51

education. Through an exploration of reform, teacher, classroom, and student
roles, this chapter inquires into the current environment of schooling.

2 Education as Solution

If education is the answer to unasked questions, as noted in Chapter 1, it also
reveals its power for change when presented as a threat to the status quo. There
is a long and ugly history in the United States of keeping people of color away
from education as a way to maintain power (Gillen, 2014; Kozol, 1991; Ravitch,
1974/2000). For example, writing about his childhood in slavery, Frederick Douglass comments that after his master discovered he had learned to read and
write, "My mistress, who had kindly commenced to instruct me, had, in compliance with the advice and direction of her husband, not only ceased to instruct,
but had set her face against my being instructed by any one else" (p. 22). Douglass had enough of a foundation to continue teaching himself, drew information from the neighborhood (white) children, and used his learning as a tool to
escape slavery. Though segregation as law formally ended in 1954, it was years
before the sluggish South did the necessary work to re-draw school communities (Ravitch, 1983) while the North became increasingly self-segregated due to
urban poverty and white suburban migration (Kozol, 1991).

It was long believed that there was little point in educating women, other
than to make them better wives and mothers. 19th century women's education
advocate Margaret Fuller-Ossoli (1855) critiques this, writing:

> The influence has been such, that the aim certainly is, not, in arranging
> school instruction for girls, to give them as fair a field as boys ... whether
> women will add to the talent of narration the power of systemizations –
> whether they will carve marble, as well as draw and paint – is not import-
> ant. But that it should be acknowledged that they have intellect which
> needs developing. (pp. 94–95)

That is, young women deserved education because they deserved to be educated. They did not need to do something amazing or groundbreaking in order
to justify their right to an education.

The poor were believed to need only minimal education to maintain basic
employment stability (Freire, 1970). In discussing the oppressor/oppressed
relationship, Freire notes, "The more the oppressors control the oppressed,
the more they change them into apparently inanimate 'things'" (p. 59). The
oppressed are never *called* the oppressed – rather, they are underdeveloped

and unrefined, in need of monitoring. The oppressors work is to keep the oppressed a docile labor force and aware of their place in society.

Young people with physical and cognitive disabilities were monitored, rather than educated, under the auspices that they could not absorb or make use of traditional classroom learning (West & National Council on Disability, 2000). It was not until 1975 that children with disabilities were guaranteed, by federal law, access to free education and appropriate services for their learning needs (West & National Council). Through 1970, over one million youth were restricted from public schools and more than 3.5 million did not receive learning support (West & National Council). Despite federal law, the practice of warehousing special-needs youth, especially those from impoverished backgrounds, continues to this day (Aviv, 2018).

Public schools in the United States are hampered with the responsibility to, among other things, teach children basic facts and information; civilize unruly bodies into a functional mass; support the development of labor; provide social services including nutrition, counseling, and basic health care; organize young people into a clearly defined progression; act as a parent/guardian during the day; recognize and address youth needs and struggles; provide space and training for subjects deemed non-academic, such as the arts and athletics; provide space and training for both advanced as well as remedial learning; effectively employ the latest technologies; provide a coherent, non-contradictory narrative of American history and the nation's standing in the world; instill an appreciation for 'fine' literature; and monitor children and young people's growth and civic participation. On the receiving end, children and young people are, among other things, expected to appreciate and respect the knowledge and expertise of their teachers and administrators; check their physicality at the classroom door; ask the 'correct' questions while not questioning anything deemed too controversial; receive their learning with appreciation; respond positively to the support provided for them; and learn the codes of what belongs in and out of school.

Just some of the myriad problems with these scenarios are that teachers are never trained in all those responsibilities; teachers and students are not automatons; not all students learn the same; and students often come to the classroom with much greater knowledge than they are assumed to possess. Left out of these scenarios is any systemic, structural effort at providing teachers or students with critical thinking and curiosity to question the larger environment in which school and education resides.

Lack of education limits opportunities. Over half of state and federal inmates did not complete high school (Wolf-Harlow, 2003). Even when inmates receive education while imprisoned, their job prospects remain seriously limited. Increased education retention can, at the very least, minimize many of society's struggles and will provide society with a competent, well-informed labor force. As of 2016, approximately 78.8% of those with Bachelor's degrees were employed year-round, earning six times as much as those who did not finish high school (Strauss, 2017). The average income for those with Bachelor's degrees was $50,000 while those who left high school was $25,900 (Back to school statistics, n.d.). Those with less formal education live in a state of constant economic recession and may have less (formal) knowledge of how to work themselves out of economic instability. Based on public opinion surveys, 77% of eligible voters with more than a high school diploma vote versus 44% of eligible voters with a high school diploma or less (MIT Election Data & Science Lab, n.d.). 78% of eligible voters making $150,000 a year vote, versus 41% of eligible voters making $15,000 a year (fairvote, n.d.).

None of these numbers speak to the *quality* of education, simply that completing increased levels of school has positive benefits on individuals' well-being. Looking 'inside' the numbers shows that high quality education is not available across all socio-economic strata. Though the national high school drop-out rate in 2016 was just 6.1% (Back to school statistics, n.d.), nearly 40–50% of students in urban districts drop out of school (Mehta, Schwartz, & Hess, 2016). Students living in poverty have the dual pressure of attending less-resourced schools, making it harder for them to move out of poverty due to lack of opportunities, as well as performing more poorly in school. Where low socio-economic status meets students of color, the "average black twelfth grader has a reading level lower than that of the average white eighth grader" (Mehta et al., 2016, p. 2). Young people living in poverty score .69 standard deviation points in math behind those not living in poverty (Michelmore & Dynarski, 2017). Students living in long-term poverty score .84 standard deviation points lower than students not living in poverty (Michelmore & Dynarski). Though more money is not always a productive solution, it is clear that *less* money creates more problems for already struggling families who bear the burden of slashed funding (Johns, Campbell, & Sargrad, 2018). Trump's education budget includes increased spending for charter schools but decreased spending on programs that support impoverished students (Richmond, 2018).

To adequately solve problems, schools need much greater support. According to Mehta (2016) real change cannot come from doing some things a bit better or slightly differently. Decades of work in the name of 'reform' have made little demonstrable change and a radical approach is needed. That radical approach can be found in multiple places. A rejection of simplistic, superficial solutions to current crises in favor of complex, carefully articulated problem-solving; comprehensive teacher education programs, addressing both theory and practice, that are not afraid to take the time or promote the skills that shape a dynamic, well-trained professional teaching force; and a concentrated effort to include the education of critical media literacy as part of comprehensive teaching education in order to integrate media literacy in the classroom and provide a conceptual frame of learning to address problem solving.

When schools are expected to solve problems without clear mechanisms to do so, schools, teachers, and students are blamed for contributing to continued problems. According to Long and Riegle (2002), "This unrealistic view of the school has contributed to the present lack of clarity about what schools should do and has complicated the process of preparing teachers" (p. xv). While Americans want good schools, there is a lack of awareness and lack of agreement of how to secure them. Since its inception, teacher education – in all its myriad forms – has been treated with indifference at best, derision at worst. For the purpose of this book, teacher education may be the starting point of change: Teachers, well trained in theories and practices of teaching, including critical media literacy, who see themselves as professionals and share relevant and dynamic instruction with their classes. With this as a classroom paradigm, the above listed responsibilities may be more clearly aligned.

It is my argument that the solution will be found through comprehensive, university-based teacher education with the required inclusion of critical media literacy. Robertson (2008) writes, "Education has been identified as both part of the cause of the current state of democratic political participation and as part of the potential solution, although where the solution lies is contested" (p. 27). The problem is not that schools/education should not be seen as the solution. Instead, if the premise that schools/education are the solution is accepted, then the route to that solution needs to be clarified and the paradigm needs to be shifted: Teachers deserve better education and that education needs to include critical media literacy. For schools to be the answer to unasked questions, the approach to teaching and learning needs to be more comprehensive. Buckingham (2007) writes:

> I believe the school could play a part in equalizing access to technology, compensation for the inequalities that currently persist in the wider society – although, in doing so, we will need to acknowledge that access is a matter not simply of technology, but also of the competencies that are required to use it. (p. 179)

That is the task at hand: To acknowledge that the acquisition of a skill or technology is bigger than the sum of its parts and requires a broader, concepts-based approach.

The K-12 school is primed to be the location and arbiter of this change. According to Buckingham (2007):

> As a public sphere institution, the school should provide a forum for open public communication and critical debate that is equally accessible to all. It should stand between the citizen (in this case, the student) and the operations of both the market and the state. (p. 182)

In a society operating under the ethos of neoliberalism, the school may be the last place that can fight back against free-market forces.

3 Location of Reform

While schooling and education are often offered as solutions, it is unclear what problem is being posed. Where policy development and reform originate and with what goals is often indistinguishable. The belief that robust policy change and thoughtful reform will make the most of education both for K-12 youth and prospective teachers runs into an immediate stumbling block when it is less clear who manages or receives what change in what environment. Buckingham (2007) writes, "reform is typically imposed by central authors, and there is little attempt to enlist teachers as collaborators" (p. 52). According to Darling-Hammond and Rothman (2015), "policymakers have typically responded to demands for school reform by focusing their attention almost exclusively on areas that have an obvious direct connection to student learning: Teacher recruitment, training, credentialing, and evaluation, as well as curriculum, testing, and accountability" (p. 25). All of these areas are ones most easily visualized and publicized – they make for rich headlines. 'Old fashioned' reform focused on teachers' unions and addressing systemic inequities (Ravitch, 1974/2000) while 'new' reform focuses on market forces, re-branding schools in the ethos of corporations (Rhee & Oakley, 2008; Fordham Foundation, 1999; Finn, 1999; Solomon, 2002), and dismantling unions (Brimelow, 2003; NPE, 2018).

The apex of concern for school reform was the release of *A Nation at Risk* (National Commission on Excellence in Education, 1983) which shared data that American youth were not performing well in school and were not competitive with global peers. According to the study, test scores were decreasing and students were not spending enough time in school or doing homework. American schools, and by extension, American society, "are presently being eroded by a rising tide of mediocrity that threatens our very future as a Nation and a people" (edreform.com). The study intimates that a threat from a foreign power – a not-so-subtle reference to Communist fears – would spark more action. Pressure is put on schools and schooling to cultivate a productive citizenry, one who can best the competition, such as the efficient Japanese automobile, the South Korean steel mill, or the German tool manufacturing – all perceived threats.

A Nation at Risk has been debunked over the years for flawed methodology and misinterpreted data (Patton, 2014). For example, because more young people across economic classes were attending school for longer periods of time, more students were taking standardized tests. The results may have been lower because it was a more representative sample of a higher number of students taking the tests (Patton). Students attending well-resourced schools saw their test scores rise. In response, a flurry of reforms were initiated post-1983, but Mehta (2016) writes that with a bit of critical distance, the reforms suggested were really minor tweaks to the same core, with an emphasis on standards, performance pay, increase in charter schools, and vague preparations for 21st century skills. In 1983, no one really knew what the year 2000 and beyond would look like, but what mattered was the appearance of forward progression and readiness for the future.

Support for reform is uneven at best. For those for whom the system of education works, there is little incentive to make change. When 78% of parents report being happy with where they send their children to school (Cookson et al., 2018), it can be easy to forget the minority who are unhappy or build incentive to change what is not working or acknowledge that just because parents profess 'happiness' does not mean the school is *good*; it might simply be better than other available options. For those in high-performing and well-resourced schools, 'the problem with schools' can easily feel like someone else's problem. Those for whom the system of education does *not* work have little power to enforce change. Home and community supports for reform are "the exception rather than the rule in most urban (and maybe suburban and rural) public schools" (Darling-Hammond, 2006, p. 5). The ability to provide support and make change is a function of the system within which schooling operates. Buckingham (2007) warns not to be too surprised by the rigidity and inflexibility of school organization and its apparent resistance to change as "these must be seen as inevitable consequences of the institutional function of the school, and of the large numbers of students it must accommodate" (p. 62). The actual reality of students' learning and teachers' work is masked by the actual reality of bureaucratic maneuverings. Teachers like Gillen (2014) work the system from within, teaching students to see that forces of economic oppression can be radically re-worked.

The United States lacks a national teacher development policy that supports the professionalization of teachers (Darling-Hammond, 2010) and reform often operates at decentralized government or industry levels, without including teachers (Buckingham, 2007) which effectively sets the tone in favor of the market rather than the community. Further, it leaves out any clarity on who checks the administrators. When looking at reform, the qualifications of administrators often do not appear to include substantial classroom work. Michelle Rhee, for example, taught for three years as a TFA fellow before moving into an administrative position (Ripley, 2008). She believed her TFA training was substandard, and yet built a teacher training program with almost the exact same model. When she was appointed Chancellor of the Washington, D.C, public schools, she had no experience as a school administrator or principal. Similarly, Joel Klein, New York City's Chancellor from 2002–2010, had zero classroom experience before taking over the largest public school system in the nation. He was trained as a lawyer and worked on behalf of corporate interests before being hired by Mayor Michael Bloomberg (Rothstein, 2012). When he left the NYC public school system, he accepted a position at Amplify, a subsidiary of Rupert Murdoch's NewsCorp, tasked with developing custom-made tablets for classroom use (Otterman, 2016). President Obama's first Secretary of Education, Arne Duncan, who served from 2009–2015, had zero classroom experience. Duncan served as a tutor, mentor, and researcher at an after-school program run by his mother before running the Chicago public school system (Wong, 2018). Current Secretary of Education Betsy DeVos has zero classroom experience, has never attended a public school, and is publicly opposed to public K-12 education (Johnson, Campbell, & Sargrad, 2018; Olen, 2018).

In a manifesto on how to fix public education, entitled "How to fix our schools," Klein, Rhee, and several colleagues (2010) write:

> A 7-year-old girl won't make it to college someday because her teacher has two decades of experience or a master's degree – she will make it to college if her teacher is effective and engaging and compels her to reach for success. (washingtonpost.com)

This will be achieved through a "performance-driven culture in every American school," an adherence to data gathering and analysis to better understand student performance, the power to close low performing schools, and, of course, replacing those low performing schools with an unlimited quantity of charter schools (washingtonpost.com). Klein, Rhee, and colleagues use President Obama's statement that the most important factor in a young person's school success is their teacher. Only, Obama never said this, exactly. He stated that the single most important *in-school* factor is the teacher. The majority of student success or struggle is attributable to non-school factors (Rothstein, 2010).

The current face of reform is dictated by billionaires taking on schooling and education reform as a side project. In 2014, Reed Hastings, the CEO of Netflix, spoke at the California Charter Association, stating, "The most important thing is that [charter schools] consistently get better every year they're getting better because they have stable governance – they don't have an elected school board" (quoted in Strauss, 2014). Hastings went on to lament California's 8% market share of charter school enrollment, well below New Orleans' 90% market share, and predicted it would be 20–30 years of work to get California that high a share. No mention was made in his speech that New Orleans is at 90% because Hurricane Katrina devastated the public schools across the city. New Orleans' charter schools perform worse than public schools and those that do perform better have selective admissions criteria (Strauss, 2014). Furthermore, 90% charter school enrollment goes against the original intent of charters to offer laboratories for innovative pedagogy (Cookson et al., 2018), a mantle which has long since been ignored. In their critique of Hastings, Burris and Ravitch (2018) write, "The objective could not be clearer: Influence districts to expand their charter sector until eventually all, or nearly all, schools are privately operated and managed ... schools become publicly funded businesses" (washingtonpost.com).

In response to the presence of billionaires' supposed interest in education, the Network for Public Education (NPE) Action (2018) published a report detailing the dollar amount spent by billionaires on education and shared nine case studies on how elections were funded to promote pro-charter school, anti-union votes. According to their report, billionaire business people funnel millions of dollars into elections, even in locations where they do not live:

> ... their agenda is to advance the privatization of public schools by whatever means necessary ... they want their allies to control state and local school boards so that more public schools will be closed and replaced by privately managed charter schools or even vouchers for religious schools. (npeaction.com)

NPE is quick to point out that these billionaires do not send their own children to public or charter schools, that they want to improve. Instead, they have a disdain for unions.

The dollar amounts are staggering. Of the top 18 billionaires donating money, some names are quite familiar: Reed Hastings, CEO of Netflix, donated $9,630,500; the Walton Family Foundation, founders and owners of Walmart, gave a total of $6,472,000; the Fisher family, founders of The Gap, gave $5,302,000; Michael Bloomberg, former NYC mayor, gave $4,361,200; the Gates Family Foundation, overseen by Bill Gates, the founder of Microsoft, gave $3,304,000; and the Jeff Bezos Foundation, overseen by the founder of Amazon, gave $1,000,000. These individuals and their family foundations are able to give so much – and relatively quietly – because of the 2010 Supreme Court Citizens United decision that equated corporations with people and permitted unlimited funding (NPE, 2018). In 2010, Facebook founder and CEO Mark Zuckerberg donated $100 million to the Newark Public School System (Perez-Pena, 2010) despite having no connection to the city or the state. Zuckerberg announced the donation on the *Oprah Winfrey Show*, alongside then-Mayor Corey Booker; both Winfrey and Booker are advocates for charter schools and school choice. The donation was considered a colossal failure because the money did not go to schools, but rather to a committee charged with making decisions on how to spend the money (Garfield, 2018).

The named billionaires have three very clear things in common: They have zero education experience; their money goes towards *elections* (not to schools or classrooms) of candidates whose choices they approve of or can manipulate; and their gifts are tax-deductible, ultimately benefitting their own bottom line. Burris and Ravitch (2018) observe:

> Billionaires live in an echo chamber of their own. As they jet across the globe to and from their many homes, the neighborhood school with its bake sales, homecoming dances and lively community elections are foreign and inconsequential. They believe the role of the average woman or man is to be a consumer, not a decider. (washingtonpost.com)

These are but a few high-profile examples of the perception that innovative, 'out-of-the-box,' market logic thinking can shift schooling.

Those involved in the classroom often have the least say in reform. TFA capitalizes on positioning well-meaning, high-achieving college students into high-risk schools, fostering a hero-complex that is not sustainable and these new teachers may have very little say in classroom or school policy. New teachers in charter schools or non-profit schools may be hired with little to no experience or training and if their focus is (understandably) on learning on the job, they may not have the tools or time to demand change from the system. Training, hiring, and retaining teachers in high-needs areas is indeed of paramount importance. Current policies and expectations do not support this in a sustainable, supportive manner, thereby perpetuating the revolving door of unhappy, underprepared, and unsupported teachers and administrators which, in turn,

60 CHAPTER 4

has a continued negative effect on the students. Countering this, the flashy headlines and popular coverage of educational policy may focus on the dire needs of urban and rural districts, which is both true and makes good copy, but Schultz et al. (2011) point out that "the reality is that for many affluent school districts, teaching positions receive an excess of applicants" (p. 6). One downside of a state-based education system is the wide variation in training, licensing, professional development, and enforcement (Darling-Hammond, 2000). Darling-Hammond (2000) writes, "In every category of possible investment in teachers' knowledge and in every area in which standards for teaching are set (e.g., licensing, accreditation, advanced certification, on-the-job evaluation), there are substantial differences in the policies and practices employed by states" (p. 12). Teaching, therefore, is not a mobile profession; even those well trained in one state may be over- or underprepared for another state, fostering less incentive by those with experience to seek out jobs where need is greatest.

4 Role of the Teacher

According to Green's (2014) popular history and guidance for teaching in America:

> The common view of great teachers is that they are born that way ... The idea of the natural-born teacher is embedded in thousands of studies conducted over dozens of years. Again and again, researchers have sought to explain great teaching through personality and character traits. The most effective teachers, researchers have guessed, must be extroverted, agreeable, conscientious, open to new experiences, empathetic, social adjusted, emotionally sensitive, persevering, humorous, or all of the above. (pp. 6–7)

Though Green herself is not a teacher, she writes an accessible, friendly guide to honing one's teaching skills. In her efforts to better understand teaching, and as part of her research, Green entered the classroom of a teacher friend to practice. She writes:

> Discussions are wonderful in theory and eyeball-yankingly difficult to facilitate in a live classroom. I had tried to arrange the lesson in three parts: modeling, to start; then individual practice working through the questions with a different text ... and finally a group discussion of what the students had learned that would, I hoped, make the specific ideas

become more abstract, taking them from what one author did to what *they* might do, if they were to write a biography of their own. (p. 318)

This was her exhausting experience for one class over the course of a few days – not multiple classes, that this book can be found in a commercial bookstore and was a bestseller reveals the underlying belief held over from the 19th century: Yes, prospective teachers need training, but just a bit, and training can be picked up, independently, from this or a comparable book. That someone who is *not* a teacher writes a *New York Times* bestseller on how to be a good teacher reveals the lack of interest for the professionalization of teaching in the United States. It buoys the neoliberal emphasis on individuals as solely responsible for their success or failure.

Historically, the idea of specialized training was deemed unnecessary, especially if prospective teachers had a competent grasp of their subject matter. In early public schooling, teachers were not meant to be innovative, creative, or respond to student needs. Instead, they were to "accept and carry out without question the rules, regulations, and curriculum guidelines laid out for them by school administrators, school board members and other policy makers, and a host of curriculum and teacher education experts" (Long & Riegle, 2002, p. xi). This begs the question: How did the administrators determine the best practices? Who determines what's 'best' and who oversees those whose job it is to oversee? 'Best practices' may be also understood as "what works," as Mehta et al. (2016) observe, "that the right mix of remedies is already known – or will soon be identified – and that the challenge is primarily a technical one of growing and transferring it" (p. 3). 'Best practices,' they note, are relative: They may bolster already successful schools with systemic advantages, but do not necessarily do much to transform "a mediocre school system into a higher performing one" (p. 4).

'Trial and error' may have been a guiding principle for far too long, leaving relationships between teachers and administrators stagnant at best and hostile more likely. When Darling-Hammond and Rothman (2015) write, "an education system can only be as strong as its teachers" (p. 27) this puts teachers in a powerful, yet precarious, position. Not nearly enough attention is paid to the complexity and difficulty of the day-to-day tasks of teachers (Darling-Hammond, 2006). The teacher's role has always been contentious and as the demand for teachers increased, market pressures on normal schools inevitably led to relaxed professional standards (Labaree, 2008). This relaxation has perpetuated and makes space for market-logic dictates: There is room to shift how teaching is understood in order to create space for professionalism in name only.

While it is clear that the teacher has a leadership role in the classroom and possibly in the school, little else is agreed upon about the role of the teacher. For Darling-Hammond (2006), to strengthen teaching and teachers, the answer lies in strong teacher education that prepares them for both the theoretical and practical of managing the classroom and teaching material. She writes:

> ... teachers work with groups of twenty-five to thirty at once, each with unique needs and proclivities. Teachers must balance these variables, along with a multitude of sometimes competing goals, and negotiate the demands of the content matter along with individual and group needs. They must draw on many kinds of knowledge – of learning and development, social contexts and culture, language and expression, curriculum and teaching – and integrate what they know to create engaging tasks and solve learning problems for a range of students who learn differently. They must balance the often conflicting desires of school boards, legislators, parents, administrators, colleagues, and students, creating a coherent community within which both learning and social growth can occur. Further, the problem of learning to teach is complicated by the common experience virtually all adults have had of school, which creates strong views among prospective teachers and members of the community alike about what school and teaching are 'supposed' to be. (pp. 34–35)

As illustrated through the lengthy quote, the work of the classroom is always dynamic, never static. Teachers may walk into a classroom with a clear lesson, but the lived experience of 25–30 students, the demands of administrators, the expectations of parents and families, isolation from or cohesion with colleagues, and their own experiences with schooling and perceptions of the learning process all enter the classroom as well. Teaching is not simply regurgitating facts in a transmission model that views the teacher as possessor of knowledge and students as willing receivers of knowledge, without obstacles or competing priorities. Freire's (1970) deconstruction of the banking model of education illuminates the destructive nature of this pedagogy and details how it serves to perpetuate oppression. Ignoring or de-emphasizing the dynamism of the classroom strengthens the banking model while depressing individual student need.

If, in fact, teachers were simply purveyors of information, which they clearly are not, their jobs would be much easier and the near-constant debates would quiet down. If teaching were so simple as the transmission of data, which it clearly is not, there might conceivably be a glut of teachers in all communities. However, it is clear this is *not* what teaching is, at least, not ideal teaching,

POLITICIZING THE CLASSROOM

and the complexities of students reveals some of the difficulties of teaching. Darling-Hammond (1999/2008) writes:

> If teachers need to be able to ensure successful learning for students who learn in different ways and encounter a variety of difficulties, then teachers need to be diagnosticians and planners who know a great deal about the learning process and have a repertoire of tools at their disposal. (p. 334)

Teachers must be able to understand their students and classrooms in the larger context of their school as well as of schooling and understand curriculum both of their own subject as well as the larger goals of curriculum progression (Darling-Hammond et al., 2005a). Darling-Hammond et al. (2005a) argue that teachers:

> ... should understand that curriculum is not static, but is continuously negotiated, and they should understand that their role as professionals is to bring an understanding of how different decisions are likely to affect student learning, identity, and future educational opportunities. (p. 172)

This is a lot to understand and manage *beyond* content knowledge and reflects the pressures of the classroom. This cannot be adequately learned in a four-six week period or without classroom practice.

The difficulties and obstacles of teaching are reflected in rates of attrition. At least 30% of teachers leave the profession within five years, with rates higher in low-income communities (Darling-Hammond & Rothman, 2015). More teachers these days are less prepared for the work of teaching (Darling-Hammond, 2010; Darling-Hammond & Rothman, 2015). Proper, in-depth teacher education will not make the act of teaching any easier, but it will provide prospective and new teachers with a greater repertoire of skills at their disposal to handle the inevitable challenges. Mehta (2016) observes that the job of teaching may be too difficult as currently envisioned. He writes, "We ask teachers to know content, to instruct 125–175 students, to take care of both their academic and social needs, as well as to prepare, grade, and handle administrative responsibilities" (p. 183).

Despite the clear complexities in teaching, the profession is bound with the assumption that the job can be done by anyone because everyone has had multiple teachers and, for anywhere from 11 –16 years, on average, had daily experience with the profession (Darling-Hammond, 2006; Labaree, 2008). Recalling the discussion of teacher professionalism from Chapter 3, students have less day-to-day experience with, for example, doctors, lawyers, astronauts, or architects and therefore do not presume any level of expertise in these fields. Mehta (2013) notes, "we let doctors operate, pilots fly, and engineers build because their fields have developed effective ways of certifying that they can do these things. Teaching, on the whole, lacks this specialized knowledge base; teachers teach based on what they have picked up from experience and from their colleagues" (nytimes.com).

Following market logic, people may pay a lot of money to access the services of a doctor, lawyer, or architect, thereby increasing the cultural cachet of the professions, whereas most students access the services of their teacher for free, making it appear less exclusive. To extend the analogy, doctors, lawyers, and architects can succeed in their profession with surly, non-compliant clients – this might result in unpleasant working conditions, but may also increase billable hours – but teachers and teaching "cannot succeed without the compliance of the student" (Labaree, 2008, pp. 298–299). hooks (2010) notes that at some point in a child's education, they stop respecting teachers, generally during adolescence, coupled with a distrust of authority figures in general. The power dynamic of teacher-student can erode the trusting relationship. hooks (2010) observes, "A major transformation will happen in our culture when teachers on all levels receive deserved regard. When teachers are revered, admired profoundly and respectfully, our ability to teach is enhanced as is the ability of our students to learn" (p. 114). That is, teachers who are well-trained and well-respected will be able to do more for and on behalf of their students, thereby strengthening understandings of the value and worth of education.

Teachers are often left out of the discussions and plans to make change in their profession and, despite working with a quantity of colleagues and students, are often isolated in their desire to make change and/or collaborate with peers, mentors, or mentees (Long & Riegle, 2002). It cannot be forgotten that to become a doctor, lawyer, or architect – or any other professional career – one must have had access to consistently good teachers, consistently good schools, and consistent opportunities for growth. Stories of people who escaped poverty via education often involved the opportunity to attend a 'better' school than what they were attending or expected to attend (Capo Crucet, 2018; Sotomayor, 2013; Toobin, 2018). The assumptions that teaching is a natural, intuitive practice, bolstered by a "a few key strategies, skills, and some technical routines" (Darling-Hammond, 2006, pp. 35–36) such as "maintaining order, asking questions, grading tests, assigning work" (Labaree, 2008, p. 299) dilutes efforts to professionalize the work.

While teaching cannot be held responsible for undoing or minimizing larger social barriers, good teaching can make a significant difference in young people's educational advancement (Darling-Hammond, 2000). Teachers' academic background and preparation, including certification status, have an impact on student achievement, with less experienced teachers and those with temporary licenses having a negative impact (Darling-Hammond, 2010). With complex, thorough education in the theories and practices of teaching, teachers may build flexible and adaptable curricula and lesson plans in ways that respect different learners and their needs (Darling-Hammond et al., 2005a). It is not simply about the transmission of data but of a nuanced understanding of the multiple social, economic, and political factors that are part of the classroom (Darling-Hammond, 1999/2008).

How teachers teach contributes to the experience of the students and their confidence in the classroom may increase with proper, comprehensive training. High profile education administrators, such as Klein and Duncan, credit great teachers for their early motivation to continue with their own educations (Rothstein, 2012; Wong, 2018). Whether these public statements are 'true' or carefully polished public relations copy, they are what we access in the press and, without direct experience, how we know these individuals. What must be remembered is that these public figures, who now promote alternative teacher training, praise teachers who were traditionally trained in education schools and were members of teachers' unions.

This praise for teachers falters when the language of their public statements is parsed out more carefully. In praise of DeVos, for example, Stossel (2018), a free-market libertarian commentator, writes, "The haters claim DeVos knows little about education, only got her job because she gave money to Republican politicians and hates free public education" (foxnews.com). He goes on to defend her choices and to obfuscate the 'free' of public schooling by pointing out how high the education budget is, but never addresses DeVos's knowledge of education or provides examples of how she is informed on education policy. Indeed, for those invested in genuine education reform, it is hard not to forget her Senate confirmation when she appeared confused by the difference between proficiency and growth. In stumbling through her answer, she stated, "I think, if I'm understanding your question correctly, around proficiency, I would correlate it to competency and mastery, so each student is measured according to the advancement they are making in each subject area," which is actually closer to the definition of growth (quoted in Wong, 2017, theatlantic.com). Her transition spokesperson, in response to follow-up questions on why DeVos could not answer the question or distinguish between two very different approaches, claimed she had been cut off (Wong, 2017). When watching the testimony, it is clear that former Senator Franken (D-MN) who questioned her on proficiency versus growth most definitely pushed her, but did not cut her off.

Classrooms and students will benefit from well-educated teachers who have a thorough understanding of theory and practice, plus a degree of self-awareness. Further, the paradigm of teaching should shift to a partnership between teacher/students with attention paid to students as heterogeneous individuals, continuous research to develop and refine best practices of approaching teaching and learning as a human endeavor, and emphasis on the morality and responsibility of the teacher (Sockett, 2001). Teaching is an inherently political act and while teachers cannot change students, they can engineer a progressive, inclusive experience for students, who themselves are also politicized.

5   Role of the Student

If the early perception of teachers was as individuals competent in their subject matter with the ability to transmit facts, the corresponding image of students was as individuals passively receptive to said facts. Students were perceived as empty vessels, waiting to be filled with knowledge, a belief that persisted through much of the 20th century (Darling-Hammond, 2006). Through the 20th century, community cohesion was seen as an outgrowth of the neighborhood public high schools (Lueck, 2018).

In many ways, schooling invented childhood and undoubtedly invented the student. Children and young people have long been a source of struggle and mystery to unravel. Buckingham (2000a) writes, "the figure of the child has always been the focus of adult fears, desires and fantasies ... children are increasingly seen as threatened and endangered ... children are also increasingly perceived as a threat to [adults]" (p. 3). Schooling and education help frame what it means to be a child or, more specifically, what it means to be dependent on adult caregivers. Contemporary constructions of childhood are largely drawn from industrialized Western nations and are relatively recent in origin (Buckingham, 2000a). Compulsory education, introduced in the 19th century, separates children from adults (Buckingham, 2000a). This separation was almost wholly created by adults, and largely exploited for the purposes of consumption (Buckingham, 2000a). Childhood and youth are not neutral categories, nor are all children – and by extension, all students – homogenous. What childhood means is dependent on social factors "such as gender, 'race' or ethnicity, social class, geographical location," a shift away from extended families to nuclear families and, increasingly, single-parent families (Buckingham, 2003, p. 21). Buckingham (2003) argues that in the changing face of childhood, "schools have signally failed to keep pace with the change" (p. 32).

The make-up and expectations of students has shifted over time. Students were never automatons, waiting passively and patiently to receive the transmitted facts and data from a (presumed) expert instructor. As schooling became more democratized, as more students started attending school, and as more schooling became increasingly necessary for professional job prospects, the student population became more diverse and, in turn, teachers taught a wider variety of learners (Darling-Hammond, 2006). Early 20th century public high schools were seen as "the people's college" because they prepared so many young people for good jobs (Lueck, 2018). Through the 1960s, a decent job could be acquired with a high school diploma. As Mehta (2016) observes, while there were clearly systemic inequalities in the public school system, these were not seen as the responsibility of schools to tackle. He writes, "Schools were explicitly in the business of sorting students, which was accepted practice. In a variety of ways, we had much lower expectations for schooling and, as a result, schools were more able to realize these expectations" (p. 181). While *schooling* may have challenged social inequities, many *schools* were positioned to reinforce inequity through perpetuation of racism, classism, and sexism. With more democratized schooling came students with more extensive needs, including learning difficulties, language learning, and family struggles (Darling-Hammond, 2006) all of which present themselves in the classroom. The United States has the highest poverty rate among industrialized nations coupled with the fewest social supports and limited classroom-based resources (Darling-Hammond, 2010), leaving struggling school children in a difficult predicament.

While standardized, transmission-model education is not intellectually stimulating for many, it is especially harmful for low-income youth of color. These students generally attend schools with fewer resources, less well-trained teachers, and inconsistent teaching and administrative staff. A "concentration of poverty" occurs in African American and Latino communities, where nearly two-thirds of students attend schools where the majority are eligible for free or reduced price lunch (Darling-Hammond, 2010, p. 36). The expansion of public schooling to include impoverished urban and rural youth further negated the professional reputation of teachers. With students from low socioeconomic status as 'clients,' teacher status is lowered (Labaree, 2008). Students of color in high-poverty areas "face stark differences in courses, curriculum programs, materials and equipment, as well as in the human environment in which they attend school" (Darling-Hammond, 2010, p. 51).

More United States' students today expect to attend college and believe that a college degree is necessary for job preparation. Yet, according to the MetLife (2011) survey of college readiness, teachers "believe that nearly half will not graduate from college" (p. 9). According to Leonhardt and Chinoy (2019), about one in three students enrolled in college do not earn a degree. Young people are *aware* that college is valuable (or, valued by society), but in their limited experience, are not clear if their school is preparing them for both acceptance to, and the ability to progress through, college.

While a majority of students believe their schools adequately prepare them for college, many teachers and parents – presumably those who have attended college and are aware of what is needed – believe that schools could be doing a better job (MetLife, 2011). Young people might also assume that acceptance to and enrollment in college is the goal, largely unaware of the work demanded upon arrival and for at least four years. In their analysis of college dropout and graduation rates, Leonhardt and Chinoy (2019) encourage high school guidance and college counselors to research not just acceptance rates to, but also graduation rates from, colleges. Students learn the requirements and expectations of 'what's next' (college or work) from their classrooms, which are not neutral spaces and may reflect the struggles or privileges of their larger community.

6 Classroom Today

Changing expectations for both teachers and students inevitably dovetails with changing roles of classrooms. While there has long been a conversation on closing the achievement gap between socioeconomic classes, Darling-Hammond (2010) notes that little attention has been paid to the opportunity gap, "the accumulated differences in access to key educational resources – expert teachers, personalized attention, high-quality curriculum opportunities, good educational materials, and plentiful information resources – that support learning at home and at school" (p. 28). In classrooms today, teachers are expected to "produce high levels of learning" (Darling-Hammond, 2011, p. 166). This is a lofty and admirable goal, but with no significant shift in the complexity of their education or professional development, may be near impossible to achieve.

Students living in high-poverty areas are unduly negatively influenced by poorly performing schools and sub-par classrooms. Alexander's (2010) astute deconstruction of the treatment of black men in the United States observes that in Chicago, young men are more likely to go to prison than to college and that as of 2001, more men were in Illinois prisons than in public colleges. In high-poverty areas, even non-poor students perform at lower levels (Darling-Hammond, 2010; Wilkinson & Pickett, 2010). Big urban comprehensive schools generally do not have the flexibility to adapt to individual student needs (Darling-Hammond, 2011). Schools and classrooms will need dramatic transformations in order to be able to support and respond effectively to all students (Darling-Hammond, 2011).

POLITICIZING THE CLASSROOM 69

Classrooms and schools, even in non-impoverished areas, suffer from decreased and tightened resources. The MetLife (2013) survey of teachers and principals found that contemporary resource allocation practices make it "very challenging for school leaders to manage budgets and resources to meet school needs" (p. 3). Classrooms and schools are expected to do more with less, which negatively influences all public schools and disproportionately negatively influences public schools in economically struggling communities. The financial stressors of reduced budgets and the need to do more with less radiates through classrooms and schools. MetLife (2013) shares that three-quarters of surveyed principals say their job, as currently enacted, is too complex and they feel acute stress several days a week. Overall, teacher and principal job satisfaction has decreased, dropping 9% for principals and 23% for teachers (MetLife, 2013). Increased job dissatisfaction engenders a negative environment in which students are trying to learn.

According to the MetLife (2013) survey, teachers want more teachers, to both reduce teacher-student ratios, and also for collaboration and community. Teachers report having very little time to work with other teachers. Teachers and principals believe students deserve more training in "higher-order, cross-disciplinary skills (such as writing, critical thinking, and problem solving), and self-motivation and team skills" (MetLife, 2011, p. 9). Though the Edison Schools work to privatize education, their teachers perceive a great deal of professional support. Edison School teachers report extensive professional development opportunities, teamwork opportunities, and clear advancement opportunities. Edison offers a "four-level career program – resident, teacher, senior teacher, lead teacher – for teacher advancement – which promotes the best to positions of greater responsibilities, professional fulfillments, and compensation, while removing the weakest from the classroom" (Solomon, 2002, p. 1327). This professional advancement comes at a cost: Teachers and classrooms are effectively re-packaged into a profit-oriented, hyper-competitive free-market business model. Generally speaking, teachers in alternative schools are not eligible for union membership and operate with limited job security.

Being a teacher, being a student, and operating in a classroom space is inherently political. According to education scholar Apple (2008):

> By its very nature, the entire schooling process – how it is paid for, what goals it seeks to attain and how the goals will be measured, who has power over it, what textbooks are approved, who has the right to ask and answer questions, and so on – is political. The educational system will constantly be in the middle of crucial struggles over the meaning of democracy, over definitions of legitimate authority and culture, and over who should benefit the most from government policies and practices. (p. 105)

Teaching and learning do not occur in a vacuum and the debates in the previous chapter must be understood in a larger context. Classrooms – those for K-12 students as well as those with prospective teachers – are not neutral spaces and the debates of the previous chapter deserve to be looked at in a larger context.

7   Conclusion

It is clear that change is imminently needed. The current face of reform weaponizes poverty, blaming those with the least for vast inequities. While this is nothing new, teachers, students, and classrooms are at a crossroads: The two major spheres of education reform are not working. 'Traditional' reform emphasizes students but does not put their needs front and center; newer, neoliberal reform, with its emphasis on hyper-individuality, pressures the individual to be solely responsible for his/her success. Both spheres are neither student nor teacher centered and both pressure a 'one-size-fits-all' ethos.

While it may seem absurd to add a new dynamic to an already fraught conversation, the inclusion of critical media literacy into teacher education may serve to shift the effectiveness of classroom reform. With its emphasis on critical inquiry drawn from conceptual learning, critical media literacy included in teacher education may be the place where concrete change can begin. Chapter 5 details how critical media literacy operates in classrooms and argues for its value in teacher education.

CHAPTER 5

Practices of Media Literacy in the Classroom

Abstract

This chapter highlights the need for teacher training, details how the inclusion of critical media literacy can benefit both teachers and students, and need not be overburdensome to include.

1   Introduction

In the film *School of Rock* (Linklater, 2003), Dewey Finn (Jack Black) is a down-on-his luck musician who, through a series of comic mishaps, ends up as a substitute teacher in an elite private elementary school. Finn, impersonating his roommate who is a trained teacher, has no teaching experience but manages to fool the principal, fellow teachers, and his students for the majority of the film. When he first meets his colleagues – who are discussing testing styles – Finn's irreverent manner illustrates how out of touch his fellow teachers are. When asked what method of testing he prefers, the hapless Finn replies, "I believe that the children are the future. Now listen, you can teach them well, but buddy, you have got to let them lead the way. Let the children's laughter just remind us how we used to be. That's what I decided long ago." His colleagues are suspicious, but remain largely unaware that he is loosely quoting Whitney Houston's (1985) song, "Greatest Love of All."

Though used for comic effect, this scene illustrates a consistent tension within teaching: How to balance expectations of traditional teaching – associated with uptight, out-of-touch teachers – with a more inclusive, student-friendly method – without appearing overly casual or uninformed. This chapter argues that the inclusion of critical media literacy into teacher education can both bridge that divide and make classrooms and curricula more relevant. With its emphasis on critical analysis and creative production, critical media literacy involves teachers and students in a shared learning environment. Because it is inherently interdisciplinary, critical media literacy invites teachers of different subjects to work together. Grounded in social justice, critical media literacy engenders students with opportunities to do work that matters to themselves and their communities. Critical media literacy learning needs to happen and can be a point of change for teacher education. For

© KONINKLIJKE BRILL NV, LEIDEN, 2020 | DOI: 10.1163/9789004416765_005

decades, media literacy scholars have argued that media literacy is necessary in classrooms (Aufderheide, 1993; Butler, 2010; Kellner & Share, 2007; Kubey, 1998; Tyner, 1998). And while this is quite true, how can media literacy operate effectively and sustainably without teachers well-versed in the subject? This chapter highlights the need for teacher training, details how the inclusion of critical media literacy can benefit both teachers and students, and need not be overburdensome to include.

2 The Need for Teacher Education

Since the early work staking the claim that media literacy was necessary for students (Aufderheide, 1993; Masterman, 1985; Moore, 1991) and the foundational work on concepts-based learning (Bazalgette, 1992; Buckingham, 2003), there has been a quiet, parallel discussion about the need to educate teachers and prospective teachers in media literacy. Media literacy curriculum and lessons cannot be inserted into classrooms as single workshops or one-off projects with any hope of sustainability (Livingstone, 2018). Until teachers are trained in critical media literacy as part of their training, media literacy will continue to struggle for classroom inclusion.

Questions of *how* to include media literacy in classrooms have been bandied about for decades. The early 1990s saw media literacy defined and codified in the United States (Aufderheide, 1993), but with little corresponding discussion of how or where to include it. Over the past 20 years, the conceptual framework for understanding questions of media literacy has been continuously refined, most recently to include social and mobile media (Buckingham, 2007). As the legislative language discussed in Chapter 1 highlights, there is a major gap in media literacy policy: It is encouraged and deemed valuable, but not required. With no corresponding funding or mandate, it will continue to languish.

If the argument in the late 1980s-early 1990s focused on the need for media literacy and the subsequent argument in the late 1990s-early 2000s focused on how and where to implement media literacy, the next challenge is how to train teachers. There is no professional career track for teachers interested in media literacy (Buckingham, 1990, 2003), thus highlighting a three-decades plus dilemma: Teachers interested in bringing media literacy to their classrooms must do so on their own, often with little institutional support. Even when teachers have administrative support, this may be fleeting, depending on the shifting priorities of the school (Butler, 2010; Butler & Ladd, 2016). Furthermore, teachers interested in adding media literacy must do so *in addition* to their other work. Because it is not something they had the formal opportunity to study while preparing for teaching, they are left to their own devices and must do so on top of, rather than built into, their other responsibilities. There are limited opportunities for media literacy credentials at the higher education level (Butler, Fuentes-Bautista, & Scharrer, 2018). Christ (2004) notes that in the United States, "the term *media literacy* is normally associated with K-12 education" (p. 92). In a small quantitative study of university undergraduates' experience with media literacy, Schmidt (2012) found, through self-reported data, that students are exposed to more media literacy at the K-12 level than at the undergraduate level and when there appeared to be courses in media studies and media analysis at the college level, they very rarely had 'media literacy' in their name. The National Communication Association (1998) saw media literacy as a "fundamental competency for literate citizens" but cannot control the implementation of this in higher education classrooms (natcom.org). A first step to including media literacy in teacher training is to make greater space for it and access to it at colleges and universities.

There are options for teacher training in media literacy, but it is rare to be offered in a teacher education program. Alternative grassroots organizations, such as the Action Coalition for Media Education (ACME), Mass Media Literacy (MML), Project Censored (PC) and the Global Critical Media Literacy Project (GCMLP) offer free and low-cost materials and workshops in critical media literacy.[1] GCMLP offers a free teacher education guide, with multiple activities designed for classroom use. The National Association for Media Literacy Education (NAMLE) offers training in employing digital technology, but because of its connections with corporate funding, does not operate independently. While rich in content, these offerings are not on a sustainable scale as part of teacher education. Teachers cannot be expected to master media literacy through limited workshops or training guides, no matter how well-intentioned. Scholars such as Baker (2012), Hobbs (2011), and Hayes-Jacobs (2014) provide training for the inclusion of media literacy through their books, but this implies that teachers are operating on their own, independently, and there is no guarantee that the lesson suggestions match their own curriculum development. These scholars are well-versed in media literacy, but what are the implications for a teacher trying to apply media literacy as learned on their own? Though well-intentioned and carefully constructed, these resources run the risk of isolating teachers further if they cannot employ the lessons collaboratively with their colleagues.

Having conducted teacher training in media literacy in various locations (Butler, 2010; Butler & Ladd, 2016), I can attest to its difficulty. Even when school administrators support the process, scheduling time in a teacher's packed schedule is difficult at best. Teachers must be willing and able to sacrifice common planning time, stay late after school hours, or negotiate coverage for missed classes. Even the most interested teachers will struggle under the constraints in their preparation and planning, including test preparation and classroom management. Even the most invested teachers struggle to find ways to connect media literacy to their subjects.

Between 2006–2008, I worked in a New York City public school, charged with building a media literacy curriculum, training teachers in media literacy, and fostering community partnership with local mainstream and independent media organizations (Butler, 2010). While the teachers were expected to include media literacy in their courses, there was no formal space to provide them with training. Professional development opportunities were limited at best. Teachers were often resistant to include media literacy because of their lack of familiarity with the subject, their limited time to add new things to their curricular scope and sequence, and their day-to-day class demands. The reality of life in a NYC high school designed for underserved, at-risk youth, often meant that curriculum advancement was de-prioritized in favor of attending to students' daily crises and emergencies. The lofty goal of theme-based learning designed to focus students' academic experience assumed that they could prioritize their academics on a regular basis. Even at a school that was designed to emphasize analysis and production of media, its implementation was stunted.

Even when teachers are interested and invested, the experience may still be protracted. In the spring of 2017, I was invited by a Western Massachusetts high school English teacher to visit the ad-hoc after-school media literacy trainings she was hosting with her colleagues. The lead teacher had an undergraduate degree in Communication and was trying to include media analysis into her classroom. She and her colleagues were looking for ways to combat personal technology use in their classrooms, to encourage good research skills, and to talk with their students about the 2016 presidential election and its aftermath. The team of teachers met once a week for several weeks and drew from materials provided for them to teach themselves about media literacy. They had a small budget, which they used to buy snacks to reinvigorate themselves after a full day of teaching. Their camaraderie was palpable; these teachers wanted to work together to make change. But even so, and even with support from their principal and the dedication to stay after school, they were isolated from any formal continuing education opportunities. This learning would be for the betterment of their classes and would not formally assist their professional development.

When professional development is formal, it cannot always be fully relevant. In the fall of 2018, I was asked to develop a 2-hour workshop for middle

PRACTICES OF MEDIA LITERACY IN THE CLASSROOM

school social studies teachers in Central Massachusetts as part of their in-service training day. The Massachusetts Department of Elementary and Secondary Education (MA-DESE) recently included media literacy as part of the 8th grade social studies unit on the development of a free press (MA-DESE, 2018). While two hours would barely allow for in-depth work, an additional wrinkle presented itself: The middle school social studies teachers looped with their students, meaning they taught 7th grade one year, then 8th grade the next year to the same group of students. Pedagogically, this gives students valuable consistency, but it makes continuing education and topical professional development difficult for teachers. Half the group I was training taught the 8th grade and could conceivably weave in media literacy for the unit. However, the in-service training day was in October and the specific unit would not be taught until March, 2019, five months after the training. The other half of the teachers were teaching 7th grade, on ancient Greece and Egypt, and therefore would not be applying the media literacy work for another 17 months. These teachers liked the idea of including media literacy in their ancient history courses, but were not sure where to begin. Furthermore, ancient history was not the topic of the professional development, echoing the concerns noted in Chapter 3 that professional development is often inconsistent with teacher needs.

When training is relevant, it still may struggle to fit into teachers' daily planning. Between 2014–2016, I worked with a colleague to execute media literacy training and curriculum development to 10th grade teachers in Central Massachusetts (Butler & Ladd, 2016). Teachers participated in several in-school training sessions, either giving up lunch, a planning period, or getting coverage for their classes (the 10th grade team had no common planning time). Teachers were provided training in media literacy and lesson plans were flexible enough to be adapted to their class progression. Some teachers never used the lessons because doing so would take away from much needed test preparation time. Some teachers adapted the lessons for other grades or classes other than for which they were intended. Nearly all participating teachers waited until the last minute (before or after the debrief day) to include the lessons. Some teachers appreciated the flexibility of the curriculum ideas while others felt that if they were going to include media lessons, they should be precisely planned out so they could insert it into the class with no modifications.

A particularly 'hot' topic may provide initial and sustained motivation for additional trainings. After the 2016 presidential election, I was asked to develop a webinar for Massachusetts librarians on evaluating news and information in the age of 'fake nown.' Over 100 K-12 and public Massachusetts librarians attended the webinar. Librarians are trained in information evaluation and resource assessment; these librarians were looking for ways to educate their students and community members on how to best assess their news media choices. This one-hour webinar sparked invitations for me, and in some cases, my students, to present in-person at K-12 school libraries and community public libraries. Over the past two years, I have visited several libraries in Massachusetts and across New England, bringing information evaluation activities and connecting with librarians, teachers, students, and community members.

Bringing media literacy to classrooms and to teachers is absolutely needed, but these examples show that it must be done more formally and with less pressure on teachers' already packed schedules. It is not sustainable when done as in-school sessions and runs the risk of being ignored or building resentment if it is an add-on to other work.

Drawing from the review of the current environment of teacher preparation and pressures in and around the classroom, it may be wildly risky to propose adding *another* element to the mix, however, as will be shown, adding critical media literacy to teacher training can go a long way to shifting the dynamic of classrooms, alter the relevancy of teaching certain subjects by including the students more actively in the relationship, and connect prospective teachers more closely with their learning and preparation.

3 Classroom Dynamics

Had the New York City teachers had media literacy as part of their teacher education, the innovative practice of a media-themed school may have been more fully realized. Had the teachers I worked with for two hours had media literacy training as part of their teacher education, they may have been able to integrate questions of media literacy into their lesson planning and the in-service day could have focused on refining their lessons, expanding their media literacy skills, or collaborating on lesson planning. Had the teachers who were teaching themselves media literacy had media literacy as part of their teacher education, they may have been able to use their after-school collaboration to co-develop sophisticated projects, across subject matters, enhancing the inter-disciplinarity of learning. Had the 10th grade team had media literacy as part of their teacher education, their time may have been less interrupted and their lessons more clearly aligned with their course progression. Had the Massachusetts librarians had media literacy as part of their education, they may have been able to support their students and community members with immediate resources and then use their spaces for more nuanced discussions and workshops.

The popular press and academic scholarship discuss regularly how students are disconnected from their classroom learning and teachers fight a losing

PRACTICES OF MEDIA LITERACY IN THE CLASSROOM

battle against personal, private technology use in the classroom. Perennial concerns about teen social media use, especially, in the United States, about sexting (Brown, El-Toukhy, & Ortiz, 2014; Montgomery, 2007; Orenstein, 2016; Sales, 2016), phone addiction (Turkle, 2011), and cyberbullying (boyd, 2014), are often matched by adults' concerns over their own self-regulation abilities (Arther, 2005; Collier, 2014). With headlines in the popular press that read "Is technology and the internet reducing pupils' attention spans?" (Jeffries, 2013), "To ban or not to ban" (Berdick, 2018), "Teen sexting: The real issue" (Cassada, 2013), and "Teenagers are sexting – now what?" (Klass, 2018), it is difficult to avoid the stress and anxiety presumed to be inherently linked with digital technology. Further, headlines such as "Smartphone detox: How to power down in a wired world" (Douclef & Aubrey, 2018) and "Top health concern for parents: Bullying, cyberbullying and internet safety" (Scheff, 2017) offer helpful tips for how to spend less time with technology and how parents can talk with their children about technology use under the guise that a bulleted 'to-do' list can shift cultural norms (The irony, of course, is these self-help guides are found online, implying that powering down and decreased internet use can happen *later*). As Schofield-Clark (2014) argues, removing the technology is not a viable solution – instead, we need to know more about the technology we are using (and why it is so tantalizing).

The flurry of data and periodic uprising of interest in such subjects may represent a deeper social concern, but it may just as easily be an enticing topic of the moment. Either way, one thing this coverage does illustrate is that the contemporary classroom is changing and analysis and practice of critical media literacy can address those changes without succumbing to moral panics (Buckingham, 1993a, 1993b). By including the concepts of media literacy, trained teachers can work their lesson plans to include the analysis and critique of popular culture, providing for students not the 'right' answer, but rather, a forum to discuss and deconstruct the complexities and contradictions of any text. For example, sexting could easily be frowned upon as wholly negative, especially (but not exclusively) for young women (Orenstein, 2016). Yet, it can also spark a conversation about body positivity/body shaming and what it means to employ the body as an object of attention. Further, discussions could include questions about privacy and ownership; depending on how the body is presented and shared, and through what platform, it is neither the subject nor the recipient of the photo that owns the image (Terms of Service, n.d.). Depending on the age/age difference between the sender/recipient, legal questions of trafficking in child pornography could be a very real concern (Stillman, 2016).

All of the above conversations could fit into a social studies class focused on law and policy, a history class focused on technological developments, an ethics course, lessons on feminist politics, or as part of a health class. For example, Jones (2018) reports on health classes, specifically for boys, that discuss pornography and how the body is represented in sexually explicit texts. In so doing, boys are able to learn the difference between simulated and actual desire and learn lessons on intimacy, consent, and sexual exploration. By drawing on young people's daily lives and having a degree of familiarity with their interests – while respecting that young people's social cultures will not and need not blend seamlessly into classroom culture – teachers and students may be able to develop a close working relationship.

One discussion throughout media literacy is how its inclusion can upend or make explicit classroom hierarchies (Butler, 2010). It would be unwise to believe those hierarchies will ever be fully erased (or that this is a good idea). Rather than attempting to erase power differentials, critical media literacy can explore those differentials. Critical media literacy can explore the accepted (if begrudgingly) power differences in classrooms and use these as a bridge to explore power differentials in media and popular culture. The vast majority of mainstream media is made by adults, who do not personally know their audiences, so are forever guessing about the correct formula for content. In mainstream media, it is virtually impossible to find content created for youth *by youth*. When young people are attracted to media that are presumed to be "theirs," a valuable conversation can result about how media get created, by whom, and for what purpose.

Social media's success – especially, as of this writing, Instagram, SnapChat, Pinterest, and Facebook – is often credited to young people's near constant use. However, they are not the creators of the platforms. Instead, young people provide a significant amount of free labor through content creation, within a carefully constructed environment. Critical media literacy does not ask young people to give up their devices or cancel their social media accounts. Rather, it encourages both young people and the adults in their lives, including their teachers, to inquire about the motivations of the corporate entities behind social media: Why are the companies making so much money when the primary users do the work for free? What are the implications when, as part of their terms of service, the owners of social media own the user's likeness and content as soon as a user posts anything? For example, according to SnapChat's terms of service, "when you appear in, create, upload, or send Public Content, you also grant SnapInc., our affiliates, and our business partners the unrestricted, worldwide, perpetual right and license to use your name, likeness, and voice, including in connection with commercial or sponsored content" (Terms of service, n.d.). Why is there so much conversation around mobile phone and social media 'addiction,' and what does it mean to employ

PRACTICES OF MEDIA LITERACY IN THE CLASSROOM

medical terminology to a social phenomenon? While social media use is presented as ubiquitous, what might be discovered when researching who is (and is not) on social media, who does (and does not) have access to high speed reliable internet access? While social media sites present themselves as 'free,' what are the larger costs associated with owning an accessible device and having Wi-Fi access? How are advertisements subtly, and not so subtly, woven into social media use?

These questions are not designed to ruin young people's (or their teachers') enjoyment of social media but rather to put it in its larger context in order to better understand it on a multidimensional level. Teaching young people about the media may very well result in no behavioral changes (Buckingham, Fraser, & Mayman, 1990; Buckingham, 1993a). Especially with social media, the only viable behavioral change is to cancel the account, which effectively leaves young people out of their (potentially) primary social environment. There is no 'a la carte' option in social media use: All of the terms of service must be wholly agreed to (including the regular updates and additions) in order to participate, itself a key topic of conversation. These terms of service are nearly impossible to maneuver. In his analysis of privacy policies, Litman-Navarro (2019) found the majority to be incomprehensible with wording that exceeded college reading level expectations, and such high word counts that it could take upwards of 30 minutes to read through each one.

One rare instance where young people were in charge of the means of production for a mainstream audience was the global March for Our Lives rallies and marches in the wake of the mass shooting at Marjory Stoneman Douglass High School in Parkland, Florida on February 14, 2018 (Burch & Mazzei, 2018; Calfas, 2018). In Washington, D.C., around the United States, and around the globe, the marches were organized, produced, and managed by young people, largely under the age of 20. In Washington, D.C., no speaker was over the age of 20 (Carlson & Patel, 2018). Prior to the march, high school students around the nation organized a 17-minute walkout to honor the 17 students killed in the attack (Yee & Blinder, 2018). The vast majority of the organizing, including promotional material and advertising, was conducted on social media, by young people. Following the marches, the youth organizers planned a summer tour to register voters, focusing on districts with politicians backed by the NRA and communities impacted by gun violence (Rozsa & Zezima, 2018). Far from demonizing social media, studying the March for Our Lives' preparation and execution highlights a positive relationship with media. Among an incredible number of teachable moments and valuable lessons learned from March for Our Lives is the reminder that young people are often more capable than they are given credit for and are far from passive or hermetically attached to their technologies. Bringing media literacy to the classroom, via conscientious teacher training, can connect students and teachers more closely to their studies, chipping away at classroom and institutional alienation. The March for Our Lives organization and execution is an example of how upending the hierarchy can have positive benefits. Young people had a motivation and exercised it to completion.

4   Subject Relevance

It is a common refrain that much of what is learned in K-12 is largely irrelevant at best, insulting at worst. A 'one-size-fits-all' approach to education does not, in fact, work for all. Though curriculum is largely based on individual state standards, that much of United States' K-12 learning falls within the white, male, Western canon (Gillen, 2014) is a genuine concern. When schools engage in 'other,' alternative curriculum, it is often a special, non-core, non-canon course. For example, when a Western Massachusetts English teacher decided to develop a class on queer literature, she did so on her own time with no additional resources (Sadowski, 2016). As the legislative language discussed in Chapter 1 illustrates, media literacy is encouraged, often as an elective, but in no way reimagines or displaces the current curriculum.

Media literacy can help support the relevancy of certain subjects by providing tools of inquiry. The conceptual approach to media literacy (Buckingham, 2003, 2007) puts any point of inquiry within a larger context, inviting both teachers and students to make more complex sense not just of what they are studying but why they are studying it. Armed with the guiding questions of conceptual media literacy learning – starting with who produced this text and for what purpose – teachers and students can work together to make their learning relevant. When students ask 'why does this matter,' they are starting the process of critical inquiry.

To teach students the continued value of research skills – even when everything, seemingly, can be Googled – is to teach how to ask questions and evaluate the data provided. When we do a Google search, how does our prior search history contribute to the results? How does the question asked contribute to the answer provided? What advertisements are we looking at when searching our results? Google has divided results into broad categories – news, images, video, maps, shopping – how do those categories frame the content of the results? Who owns Google and what does Google own that might receive greater attention? Is there anything that *cannot* be Googled? While we are searching Google, what is Google searching about us? It is a poorly kept secret that Google

PRACTICES OF MEDIA LITERACY IN THE CLASSROOM

monitors all our searches, reads all our emails, and gains access to the data of people *without* Google emails who have contacted Gmail users (Goodman, 2015) and yet many of us continue to use the site and its services because it is convenient, consistent, and feels reliable. Because of the algorithms associated with our search histories, what we find when we search matches our worldview so we are rarely challenged to think anything new or different.

Critical media literacy can help teachers organize research projects to evaluate the quality of material found through research, while also exploring the research tool as an object of study. When the middle school social studies teachers teaching ancient history asked me how to make their topic relevant to media literacy work, we discussed forms of communication, art, entertainment, and how people shared information. With a willful suspension of disbelief and a manipulation of time and technology, how would the ancient Greeks and Egyptians use Instagram? What information and images would they relay? What pictures would they share, with what filters? What would be the content of their Snap Stories? How would they express their political views, or might that be forbidden? How would they announce an event and curate a guest list? Who would have what access to the latest technologies?

Students and teachers can make ancient history, or any other topic, relevant with a little creativity; to answer any of the above questions, students will have to do research on the people and the time period, including who had power and by what means they exercised it. By maneuvering through the narratives of the past, students will be able to construct a picture of what life was like and, through their own present-day understandings, connect the subject to their daily lives. No subject needs to be presented to students as pre-packaged or already decided upon prior to their learning of it. Through critical analysis, young people are invited to see that all stories are constructed and can be re-imagined.

Furthermore, applying critical and creative production can engage students more fully in their learning. While there are critiques that work in production runs the risk of mimicking mainstream media (Lewis & Jhally, 1998), other arguments highlight that through construction of media, young people gain a better, more nuanced understanding of how media are produced and distributed (Buckingham, Sefton-Green, & Grahame, 1995; Grahame, 1991). When students make media, especially for a real audience, they see their work through a different lens. Teachers and students who utilize GCMLP, or write Verified Independent News Stories (VINS) through Project Censored, publish their work on the sites, thereby adding the element of a real audience to student work. While most student work remains in the confines of the classroom, read primarily by the teacher and possibly by classmates, publishing student work

82   CHAPTER 5

via GCMLP or Project Censored invites students and teachers to have their work read by an audience of strangers, not unlike their own role as audiences of mainstream media.

5   Connecting Teachers

Including critical media literacy education in teacher preparation may connect teachers more thoroughly to their own process. If the argument that comprehensive teacher education should include both theoretical development of subject mastery as well as pedagogical awareness of classroom management, critical media literacy can weave those strands together.

Media literacy has a rich theoretical history, tied closely to teacher and classroom experiences (Buckingham, 1990, 1993a, 1998a; Buckingham, Fraser, & Mayman, 1990; Buckingham, Grahame, & Sefton-Green, 1995; Buckingham & Sefton Green, 1994; Grahame, 1991; Masterman, 1980, 1985). Practitioners of empirically grounded media literacy work have worked directly in classrooms, with teachers and students, to better construct the practical work of media learning (Butler, 2010; Goodman, 2003; Scharrer, Olson, Sekarasih, & Cadrette, 2016). Teacher education research has explored ways to not add *more* superfluous work to teachers' schedules, but to make it part of what they are already doing. Organizations like Project Censored make it possible for teachers and students to co-publish work through their VINS. School-based programs such as the Educational Video Center (EVC) and after school programs like Global Action Project (GAP) work with teachers and students, to provide practical training in video production. Projects such as See-Hear-Feel-Film (SHFF) provide students with visual literacy skills and teachers with classroom activities to enhance their learning (Butler, 2015). If any of the above could happen more systematically *while* prospective teachers are being educated, they, in theory, could work the material in their courses instead of having them as additions or special one-time projects.

6   Justification for Practice

In 1991, Moore proposed curriculum ideas across subject matters that infused media literacy learning into curricular planning. He writes, "If media education is to become a term within the new curriculum initiatives, then the extension of ideas and strategies from media studies 'across the curriculum' into all subjects and disciplines is important" (p. 171). While a significant amount of work has been done under the umbrella of media literacy since

PRACTICES OF MEDIA LITERACY IN THE CLASSROOM

1991, work in its name must still be justified and there is still a great deal of confusion about how to include it across the curriculum. In my own experience (Butler, 2010; Butler & Ladd, 2016), teachers across subject matters struggle with how to include media literacy in their lesson plans, even when they know it is important and respect its value. When teachers are educated in a particular subject, it is understandable that an *additional* subject on top of that may be considered threatening or distracting in some way. In addition, because many teachers are under so much pressure to 'teach to the test,' it is difficult to ask them to do more. While they may desire a more creative, inclusive approach to teaching, they may also be boxed into a highly restrictive curricular plan.

While including media literacy across the curriculum is challenging, it need not be an insurmountable task. Moore (1991) detailed specific projects that could be done in multiple courses and illustrates how specific subjects can employ media literacy:

> *English:* The most obvious place where media literacy rests is in English courses because of the connections to critical thinking and textual analysis. Media literacy could bring "attention to publishing institutions, the ways in which literature is written, circulated and marketed, as well as the relationship between these institutions and established notions of literacy value" (Moore, 1991, pp. 181–182). This is one area where media literacy can move beyond content representation and address the 'behind the scenes' work of the means of production.

> *Art:* With its emphasis on the visual, art courses might also be considered a logical home for media literacy curriculum (Moore, 1991).

> *Geography, History, Sciences, Mathematics:* Much of what we learn about the world is learned through our media. Geography, history, the sciences, and mathematics are clear examples of this. Students learn about different cultures and geographies, plus points in history, both through current media's retelling of stories as well as how the media of the time addressed the issues in question as current events. Exploring the dominant media of the past and how stories are told can help young people understand both the structure and organization of their present media as well as how to envision history through the lens of the media.

> *Mathematics:* Mathematics is a sign system with its own language (Moore, 1991) and the media consistently share with audiences numbers that are deemed significant or damning. Critical media literacy can serve to deconstruct those numbers, their representation, and their institutional position.

84 CHAPTER 5

Sciences: Understandings and value ascribed to science are filtered through the media; critical media literacy can help detangle scientific messages. Furthermore, the work of textual analysis can help evaluate the research, documentation, and presentation of scientific and mathematical principles. Scientific advancement is rooted in asking questions – critical media literacy is grounded in critical inquiry, a similarity between the two.

Critical media literacy is inherently steeped in social justice work, asking its participants to look for ways to make change in their communities. Moore (1991) notes that media literacy can contribute to anti-racist work in "helping to understand not only *what* parts images play in constructing 'ourselves' as different from, even superior to, 'others' but also *how* they do this" (p. 180). To justify critical media literacy is to acknowledge that we see the world largely through the media, both from our own role as audience as well as how the media construct narratives.

7 Conclusion

This chapter argued for the importance of media literacy in the classroom, but that is only part of the story. Ideally, media literacy education is not a single, stand-alone class or even a series of classes. Media literacy is woven in and among all subject matters – but more so than this, it is woven in in a way that it becomes a way of developing our worldview. How we see the world, once we have been educated through the lens of comprehensive, critical media literacy, may have a profound impact on the world.

Another key part of this story is asking how this will happen. Schools and schooling already have an incredible amount of responsibility, how it is fair or equitable or responsible to ask them to take on *more* responsibility? What I am asking is that schools take on more *clear* responsibility, which may involve questioning what is available to them and how to incorporate the new responsibility more efficiently. Chapter 6 details the core of media literacy and how work in its name can alter the execution of education.

Note

1 In the interest of full disclosure, I direct and/or sit on the board of these organizations.

CHAPTER 6

Conclusion: (Media) Education *Is* the Answer

Abstract

This chapter discusses the value of critical media literacy as part of education reform and argues for the inclusion of critical media literacy in teacher education. This chapter details how this can happen and what value it may add to classrooms and the teacher-student relationship.

1   Introduction

Edward R. Murrow secured his place in history as an incorruptible investigative journalist. Laura Ingalls Wilder went on to have a rich and complex life as a farmer and, ultimately, an author. *The Onion* is in no danger of running out of information to mock and satirize. Dewey Finn inspired students to the best talent show performance ever. These teachers and media figures of past and present, from fiction and non-fiction, can teach us a lot about media literacy. Why are these texts produced and what makes them entertaining? What is our responsibility as audiences of these texts? That is, how do we interpret their narratives and understand their language in order to comprehend their meaning? By exploring texts that address education, what is learned about teachers, students, and classrooms? How can both fiction and non-fiction media help us understand classrooms, students, and teachers? How can satire and mockery help us see larger truths? What is the value of creative thinking when coupled with traditional education? What responsibility do the media industries have in telling 'accurate' or fantastical stories? While many of us have lengthy experiences with education and teachers, what can be learned from engaging with media about education?

This chapter defends critical media literacy as a site for education reform with a simple demand: Include critical media literacy in teacher education. It is clear that media literacy is necessary and that bringing media literacy into classrooms is needed. Bringing media literacy to classrooms is a goal, not the starting point. If media literacy in classrooms is the starting point, it will continue to be met with disappointment and frustration. I am choosing a new starting point: Teacher education. Admittedly, this is itself an arbitrary starting point; an argument could be made that media literacy is its own topic and

© KONINKLIJKE BRILL NV, LEIDEN, 2020 | DOI: 10.1163/9789004416765_006

86 CHAPTER 6

instead of training prospective teachers of any subject how to include media literacy, one could argue that the media literacy teaching profession needs to be cultivated to develop media literacy as its own subject area.

2 Many Calls to Action

In Mehta et al.'s (2016) introduction to their edited reader on radical school reform, they preface their plan with the observation that "ideas have consequences" (p. 3). In outlining the chapters to come, they warn, "this is not a book for the faint of heart" (p. 11). These two qualifications struck me as valuable preparation for reading their text and, at the risk of hubris, I would like to borrow them to close out this book.

Generations of minimal, piecemeal reforms have done little to change schooling. Increased money, privatization, standards, testing, small schools, vouchers, charters, longer school days, and increased time in schools have resulted in little demonstrable change. Public schools are a key part of American democracy and public schooling is at risk of private takeover by for-profit and non-profit corporations, many of which are directed and staffed by administrators with zero educational experience. Many high-profile educational reformers and those in positions of great corporate power with an interest in changing the face of education argue in favor of charter schools and alternative teacher training despite their lack of experience in classrooms in part because of their faith in the free market and a desire to re-make schooling in the private interest. The free market harms those with minimal access to it, thereby further compartmentalizing those with less privilege and fewer opportunities. The quiet, financially powerful movement by billionaires includes donating to political campaigns to change the face of public education from within, shifting it to a private model and increasing the quantity of charter schools. School is touted as the most reliable route out of poverty – but if young people and their families cannot access quality schooling, poverty remains. Furthermore, schools are not businesses and re-making public schooling into a business model considerably changes the work of school.

Over the years, there have been many efforts at education reform, many of which are variations on what is already in place. From the top down, successive presidents have enacted changes to public school education, including teacher education, that they have presented as major overhauls. Upon closer examination, they are only minor changes that have left schools relatively stagnant and schooling relatively unchanged. Presidents Nixon and Reagan heeded Friedman's (1955) suggestion for more vouchers and charter schools.

CONCLUSION: (MEDIA) EDUCATION *IS* THE ANSWER

President Carter's willingness to spend resources on progressive education was quickly cancelled by President Reagan (Tyner, 1998). President Clinton put more computers in classrooms, but without corresponding support (Tyner, 1998). President Bush enacted No Child Left Behind (NCLB), which measured test scores as evidence of success (Ravitch, 2010). President Obama lifted many of NCLB's most stringent requirements, but its replacement, Race to the Top, illustrated an adherence to free-market principles (Howell, 2015). The current administration's Secretary of Education Betsy DeVoss is publicly and proudly opposed to public education, and possesses little knowledge of it (Olen, 2018; Wong, 2017).

From the ground up, students have worked to stake their claim in schooling, resisting or accepting the policy changes. Exemplified through *Brown* vs. Board of Education (Ravitch, 1983), students and the communities of which they were a part refused to accept substandard learning. Over the years, students of color (Alonso, Anderson, Su, & Theoharris, 2009), students of poverty (Anyon, 2014; Gillen, 2014), queer students (Sadowski, 2016), and students with learning disabilities (West & National Council, 2000) have fought for greater access to quality schooling. Teachers and scholars have worked to change the execution of schooling to include greater attention to the mutual relationship between teacher and student (Freire, 1970) and to explore student-responsive methods (Delpit, 2002; hooks, 2003, 2010; Kohl, 2002).

However, these students, their families, and teachers live in a neoliberal environment that rewards hyper-individuality, competition, and blames students, families, and teachers for individual failure without attention to structural inequity. They are fighting an uphill battle, often with limited information about the forces working in favor of neoliberalism. Presented with enticement such as 'choice' and promised the best teachers, it is hard not to be drawn to these options. However, beneath the catchy language and polished marketing materials, these 'choices' often serve to harm students and their families. When billionaires are giving millions of dollars for the campaigns of candidates in favor of unfettered charter school growth and anti-union measures (NPE, 2018), 'choice' is not a genuine option, but rather an industry myth.

Teacher training in media literacy is not a short-term solution and it will not happen quickly. Livingstone (2018) writes:

> Media education is a long-term solution – it takes thought-through pedagogical strategies and years of teaching, not a one-shot campaign. It needs investment in teacher training not branded messaging. It should be evaluated in terms of learning outcomes, not simple measures of reach. (blogs.lse.ac.uk)

As potential teachers are learning the craft and art of teaching, they will also learn the analysis and production of media and how to work this into their subject and/or classroom teaching. Teachers well-versed in critical media literacy can bring it into their subjects and classroom work, thereby engendering a media literate youth. Media literate youth, in turn, may make more informed choices and will have the skills to engage in the process of continuous critical inquiry, thereby shifting their participation in the larger culture.

In terms of education reform, there have been many calls to action over the generations, many of which have changed the face of schooling – such as opening schools to women, students of color, the poor, acknowledging the standpoint of queer youth, and those with cognitive and physical disabilities, for example – while many have done little to progress schooling forward for anyone but those in already privileged positions. Including media literacy in teacher education may have consequences, both planned and unforeseen. The work of including media literacy in teacher education is not for the faint of heart. It is, however, necessary.

3   Teacher Education in Critical Media Literacy

If we continue to put media literacy in classrooms without teacher education, it will continue to swirl in confusion. We need a new starting point. I believe the new starting point should be located in teacher education programs. Those training to be teachers deserve at least one comprehensive course (ideally, more than one) grounded in the theories and practices of critical media literacy. Teachers deserve more than one-shot or short-term workshops for their own training or those brought into their classrooms for their students. Prospective teachers deserve conceptual learning that focuses on production, audience, language, and representation (Buckingham, 2003, 2007) and incorporates work on both the content of media as well as the means of production. They deserve to have the ability to address the latest trends in popular culture as well as how to make use of well-established media to inform and bolster their subjects.

Ultimately, what is being asked is that universities with education schools and teacher training programs affiliated with universities update their course offerings to include undergraduate and graduate courses in media literacy. This can happen through students requesting curricular updates to include media literacy and faculty offering to teach courses in media literacy. Media Studies programs and departments of Communication need to highlight their media analysis, media criticism, and media literacy courses and open them

CONCLUSION: (MEDIA) EDUCATION *IS* THE ANSWER

up to a variety of students. Media analysis is itself interdisciplinary and will benefit a wide variety of students. University administrators concerned with the revenue expense of offering new courses may be placated with the revenue enhancement of drawing in new students. Administrators need to provide resources to support the inclusion of media literacy courses. I am under no illusion that this can happen overnight or right away – and will take work to develop courses and include faculty with the skills to teach the courses. But the long-term goal is clear: Well-educated prospective teachers will bring greater expertise and more adaptable tools and skills to their classrooms, engendering a more media literate populace overall (and, in the long term, bringing better prepared students to the colleges and universities that trained their teachers).

This is both enticing and terrifying. It is enticing because a more media literate populace may make more informed choices. It is terrifying because this more media literate populace may choose to fight back against neoliberalism, may demand political and social change, may demand content and production change from media industries – or may do nothing at all. Doing nothing at all may be one of the consequences. It is my estimation that this is worth the risk. If a more media literate populace *does* fight back against the system, this will terrify the media conglomerates who may see their power and control dissipate.

4 Does Media Literacy Work?

To include media literacy in any capacity is to assume, on a certain level, that it works. While a small number of quantitative studies illustrate that media literacy interventions change behavior on a limited level (Bikham & Slaby, 2012; Fingar & Jolls, 2013; Joeng, Cho, & Hwang, 2012), this is still a great deal of pressure on a solution that does not have a clear place in the larger culture. A great number of analytic studies illustrate the value of media literacy as an intellectual endeavor (Frechette & Williams, 2016; Jhally & Earp, 2013; Rubin, 1998; Kellner & Share, 2007; Macedo & Steinberg, 2007; Potter, 1998; Tyner, 1998) and a respectable number of ethnographic and empirical studies show how media literacy operates on the ground, in classrooms (Buckingham, 1990; Buckingham, Fraser, & Mayman, 1990; Buckingham & Sefton-Green, 1994; Butler, 2010; Goodman, 2003; Scharrer et al., 2016). Scharrer (2002) observes, "Just as exposure to media is but one (important but not individually operating) factor shaping our Ideas, views, and actions, participation in a media-literacy curriculum is only one factor to weigh against a multitude of others in determining a person's susceptibility to media effects at any given point in time" (p. 356). Media literacy is not a panacea and one thing cannot be solely responsible for multiple changes. Possibly more important, by measurable standards, the goals of media literacy remain largely unclear. More research needs to be conducted on the goals and outcomes of media literacy work, especially in determining what media literacy competency looks like. For traditional protectionists, a goal is to turn off the media, but this is largely unrealistic in our current media environment. For celebrationists, a goal is to harness the creative prowess of young people as they use technology, but this often ignores the context wherein the media or technology of choice resides.

The primary goal of media literacy should *not* be to change behavior. Equating success with behavior change will certainly be a dismal disappointment not least because it is not feasible in the current mediated landscape for young people to wholly disconnect from media. Further, measuring the effect or impact of media literacy education may remain an elusive task. Students of media literacy may have an 'ah-ha' moment well after the theories were initially taught. The pieces of data that make up awareness may be a continuous process of discovery where bits and pieces are learned, re-learned, and refined over time.

Media literacy learning is not so much encapsulated in a singular class or series of classes but rather, in developing a worldview grounded in continuous inquiry and once that is open to regular exploration. Maybe young people would benefit from less screen time, but in order to make this a long-term behavioral change, it must be their decision to make, not one handed down by adults, however well-meaning. Maybe when young people see how their time and attention is manipulated by social media, the pressure to be always on, always connected, they might choose to disable their accounts – but maybe not. Social media is a primary form of socializing for young people, so it is entirely possible that the industry manipulation is less of a concern than their peer group connections. Furthermore, 'less screen time' also needs to address expected screen time on schoolwork, which is becoming increasingly digitized. Silicon Valley technology leaders may have the luxury to remove technology from their children's home lives, but their professional work to bring technology to classrooms means that it is something that needs continued attention. Buckingham (2011) writes:

> The primary aim of media literacy education is not to reduce the influence of 'bad' media or advertising, any more than the aim of literacy education is to reduce the influence of 'bad' books. Rather, it should be seen as part of a more fundamental rethinking of how we teach about culture

CONCLUSION: (MEDIA) EDUCATION *IS* THE ANSWER

and communication in a world that is increasingly saturated with commercial media. (p. 229)

We live in a commercial media environment *and* a commercial education environment; media literacy can teach us more about both these spaces, with more and better informed young people and teachers working together. Exploring these systems from within may serve to change them over time, bringing both education and media back from hyper-privatization.

In addition, what a media literate person 'looks like' needs greater clarification. If a young person is media literate, do they engage less, or possibly more, with the media? If a young person can identify racism, sexism, homophobia, classism, ableism, and corporate power in media, is the expectation that they will change their media choices? Maybe the media literate teacher and student spend *more* time with the media, critically assessing both the content and the means of production and, through that process, have greater material with which to 'talk back' to the media, or create new and different media, or have a more thorough understanding of themselves, their history, and how they fit into society. Maybe the media literate teacher and student who identify racism, sexism, homophobia, classism, ableism, and corporate power in media will have a more informed understanding of the choices they are making and might better recognize texts that work against these messages. Maybe the media literate person recognizes the contradictions inherent in their choices and works to make different choices – or, acknowledges that contradictions exist and work to minimize them.

It is also entirely possible that the media literate person makes no changes beyond a cognitive shift in awareness. In order to engage in the process of critical inquiry and to engage in social justice action, media cannot be ignored or 'turned off;' they must be regularly addressed. This introduces a conundrum inherent to media analysis: To analyze the media is to pay it attention. To pay attention to media is to give it credibility and normalize its narrative on some level. To analyze media is to accept it, on some level, even if it is critiqued and criticized. Independent media literacy groups, such as Project Censored, ACME, MML, and GCMLP refuse corporate funding under the premise of autonomy and independence, yet still must use the tools of mainstream media – including Facebook, Instagram, and Twitter – to get their message out. If I use a clip from a movie in my class, I am giving that movie some level of credence. Even if I am teaching a critique of the movie, by drawing from the clip (possibly via a streaming service), I am adding to my own digital footprint and sending information that, on some level, the movie is worth my time and, quite possible, my money. Turning off the media limits our learning. Engaging with media may be inherently contradictory. That bind is itself a topic of study within critical media literacy.

5 What Is 'Good' Media Literacy?

Buckingham argues repeatedly that media literacy inclusion is the solution to many current educational struggles. He also warns that we need to be cautious about applying too much credit to media literacy. He writes:

> Perhaps, above all, we need to understand a great deal more about what makes for good practice in media education – and ultimately about whether it actually makes a difference ... Is media education effective, not so much in enabling students to pass exams, but in the sense that it influences what happens outside the classroom, in their everyday engagement with media? (2007, p. 174)

That is, media literacy will not necessarily make students better test takers or a better fit into the standard model of classroom learning. Instead, media literacy asks practitioners to up-end and alter the system. The content and structure of public schooling has changed minimally in the United States in generations. The inclusion of media literacy could radically shift this, changing the act of schooling in ways currently unimaginable.

There is plenty of *bad* media literacy out there and available for teachers. Google's foray into digital literacy (Singer & Maheshwari, 2018) is but the latest in a string of corporate efforts to develop media literacy. The technology companies that provide 'free' technology and lessons on how to use their products operate under the guise of media literacy learning. Reviewing the history of media literacy in the United States, Jhally and Earp (2003) trace a vicious circle of conservative politics that beat back efforts at structured critical analysis, resulting in media education efforts that "now fit well enough within the demands and logic of the commercial media industry to win its approval and funding" (p. 13). Corporate media embraces media literacy and, indeed, funds media literacy initiatives to better understand their audiences as a means to increase consumption. Media literacy need not be responsible for eradicating or upending capitalism, a task better left to other fields. However, critical media literacy is in a position to confront capitalism and bring to light the primary goal – massive profit of the multinational corporations who, by stint of their small number, stand to absorb even greater profits. These corporations are not shy about their desire for profit and media literacy scholars are not immune to this desire, either (Yousman, 2016).

CONCLUSION: (MEDIA) EDUCATION *IS* THE ANSWER

It is not just corporate media entities that embrace the logic of the free market. Media literacy practitioner Hobbs argues the only way to make media literacy mainstream is to accept corporate funding (Ingles, 2001). Referencing her work in the 1990s, Hobbs believed that cable television companies could advance media literacy work and she felt "really warm and fuzzy" about the relationship potential, including harnessing their money and reach (Jolls, 2011, p. 7). What goes unsaid is how she stands to profit from this relationship as well. Hobbs defends her relationships with corporate media and expressed surprise when these choices were criticized. She found it hard to be critiqued by those who took umbrage at her work to seek corporate funding, saying, "as someone who loves to be loved, this was a difficult period for me professional and personally" (Jolls, 2011, p. 8). Hobbs has been funded by Channel 1, The Discovery Channel, Nickelodeon, and Google to study their work and develop curriculum on their behalf.[1] The National Association for Media Literacy Education's (NAMLE) conference and their Media Literacy week initiatives are sponsored by mainstream media corporations, including Nickelodeon and Twitter (namle.net, n.d.). By partnering with corporations, especially those that constantly monitor their users' activities, work done in media literacy's name becomes diluted. Hobbs may be correct that the only way to make media literacy mainstream is to partner with corporations – but in doing so, there are consequences. If media literacy becomes a tool of private industry, it succumbs to the neoliberal ethos. If a goal of media literacy is critical autonomy, can media literacy with corporate connections foster autonomy? Media literacy is the tool that can bring public education back from the brink of privatization, but not if media literacy itself is privatized.

What is needed is *good* media literacy: Theory and practice that advances independent, critical thinking and action through analysis and creative production of a variety of texts, with reflective work built into its structure, in curricula across subjects and grades, infused into classes. I argue that to enact 'good' media literacy, one must embrace *critical* media literacy. Critical media literacy need not change behavior, but rather, invites young people to think about their own media choices beyond the walls of the classroom. Bringing their own interests to the classroom, foregrounding their inquiries and curiosities can make more challenging topics relevant and highlight connections between course content and subject interest. And just like we are not audience to *all* media, classroom work in media literacy can show us that we need not love every topic or every class in order to learn from it. Critical media literacy does not ask young people or their teachers to stop texting, stop surfing, stop watching, or stop posting. Instead, it asks teachers and students to work towards a more nuanced understanding of why these activities feel so fulfilling and so necessary. Possessed of critical media literacy, a Netflix binge day, scrolling through filtered Instagram pics, or sharing a series of SnapStories can be both entertaining *and* educational. If young people choose to alter their behavior – watch less TV, play fewer video games, shut down social media accounts, for example – they do so of their own accord, based on their own informed decision making, not because an adult who supposedly knows better told them to. In addition, if young people choose *not* to change their behavior, to continue to make consistent use of mainstream media, they do so with the full knowledge of the content and context of their choices.

Critical media literacy also tackles the hard work of interrogating what is *not* there or what appears *unknowable*. In critical media literacy learning, the absence of data is data. Studying the stories that are told is one layer of learning. Media literacy also invites an inquiry into the stories that are not told: Who is consistently missing from our mediated stories? What stories are *not* being told? Whose stories are compartmentalized into particular roles or messages? What can be learned from exploring what is missing from popular, mainstream narratives? When looking at media content, there is a notable absence of women, people of color, queer people, and differently abled bodies. Who produces and distributes media and how can their identities help illustrate what is *not* visible in content? Why are terms of service and privacy policies so incredibly challenging to sift through? What is the benefit to the corporation when we sign up for social media sites, accept cookies on websites, or give away our information without knowing exactly to whom?

Independent, critical media literacy has the potential to wrestle public schools back from the brink of private takeover. When teachers and students are invited to question what is presented to them, they may parse out the harmful language and policies aiming to destroy the 'public' of public schooling.

6　How to Do It?

To begin the process of bringing critical media literacy into teacher education, it should be approached as a media literacy project, as detailed through the concepts of media education:

> *Production: Who are the producers of the narratives and what is their goal? How are the narratives constructed?*
> The two dueling narratives between traditional and alternative teacher education share the goal of getting more teachers into classrooms. Traditional teacher education's narrative focuses on time to learn both theory

and practice in order to enter dynamic classrooms with greater preparation. Alternative education's narrative capitalizes on the lure of the free market directing money spent on public education and shifting it to charter schools. The narratives are constructed using language and messaging that promises to solve the other side's problems: Traditional teaching training will put highly qualified teachers in classrooms and strengthen a system that, at its core, is effective and inclusive. Alternatively trained teachers will bring a youthful energy or a degree of business acumen, both lacking from traditional programs. Alternatively trained teachers, especially in charter schools, will be able to exercise innovative ideas.

The 'behind the scenes' of these narratives reveal a deeper, less publicly palatable, truth: Traditional teacher education is outdated in its belief that public schooling works for all; the 'one-size-fits-all' model is largely untrue. Further, traditional education reformers are part of the neoliberal efforts to emphasize the might and righteousness of hyper-individuality. Conversely, alternative teacher education is not really about innovative pedagogy or more flexible schooling but rather about the profit margins of those running the alternative programs and the dismantling of public institutions and the systems of support, such as teachers unions, in order to fully embrace a private, exclusionary system.

Language: What familiar codes and conventions make meaning clear?
Both positions capitalize on inclusive language, drawing in their constituents. Traditionally trained teachers have pedagogical stability and the support of expert faculty connected to research in higher education institutions; all of this sounds and feels stable. Alternatively trained teachers are primed to support choice and a new way of doing things, which sounds ripe for and capable of quick, efficient, innovative change. This language is echoed in the popular press. We learn very little about the actual functioning of Boards of Education – information deemed dry and overly bureaucratic – while we learn a lot about individual schools, teachers, or administrators who are doing spectacular, or spectacularly awful, work. A regular, mostly effective school is not worth the time or attention of the popular press. Average kids, attending functioning schools, where things go (mostly) according to plan, do not attract our attention. If we choose to search for political contributions, we are faced with extraordinarily high dollar amounts that are donated specifically to change the face of public education to the private interest.

96 CHAPTER 6

Representation: What events are utilized to create the story and how are we invited to see the world in one way (and not another)?
The successes or failures of classrooms and teachers make for good visuals and can be uplifting or can be concerning, but either way, are a call to action. The appointment of a highly visible administrator creates a story that may or may not cohere with the hiring of certain teachers or the success/failure of certain students. Our entertainment media capitalizes on these stories of individual teachers who save students' lives or individual students who give teachers' purpose. Our entertainment media embellish these stories for profit. Meanwhile, we all carry with us our own story/ies of education, which frame how we view the stories we watch, read, or listen to in the popular press.

Audience: Who is targeted and who is paying attention to the story?
We have all had teachers, some of us may be teachers, some of us may train teachers, some of us may be training as teachers, and some of us may be parents whose children have teachers. Some of us might have a side interest in education or are curious about education and are confused about all the conflicting data. Some words – such as 'choice,' 'accountability,' and 'standards' – appear great, but might feel suspicious because they do not appear to answer: Whose choice? What choice? Accountable to what? Accountable to whom? Standards determined by whom? Standards to determine what? The target audience is extraordinarily broad – it might not be an exaggeration to say 'the nation' – and how they are reached will compartmentalize them. In the neoliberal arena where individuals are rewarded for their success and punished for their failures, an audience member who is confused by the media messaging may internalize that confusion and blame themselves for their lack of understanding. It may be just as likely that there is a concerted effort to obfuscate information so that audiences do not have a clear line of available data from which to gather and organize their thoughts.

7   The Manifesto's Journey

At the outset if this book, I employed two metaphors that I would like to address more directly now: I claimed this book was a manifesto for including critical media literacy into teacher education and that the organization of the book was designed to take readers on a journey. My intention with the manifesto is to declare that training in media literacy is needed and can be a

CONCLUSION: (MEDIA) EDUCATION *IS* THE ANSWER

site for progressive change in teacher education, classroom reform, and our worldview. I am under no delusion that this will happen right away, which is why this is a journey. I hope the journey laid out in these pages illustrates the value of media literacy while also showing that how media literacy education is currently envisioned reveals a lack of sustainability. In addition, I hope I have made the case for *critical* media literacy that neither blames nor praises media, but rather, endeavors to understand the media in context, to remain independent in analysis, and to pay attention to the means of production. Media literacy cannot accept corporate funding to engage in analysis or curriculum development and still claim independence. Students, teachers, and school systems have enough uphill battles and in the age of neoliberalism, corporate benevolence is tempting but ultimately, too great a risk. Public schools may be the one public institution that can wrestle their way out of corporate control and private interest. Critical media literacy in teacher training can support this work through engagement with difficult questions. Through the lens of critical media literacy, *the answer* may be less important than the process of continuous critical inquiry.

I do not pretend this change will happen overnight. What I am asking is that teachers, prospective teachers, school administrators, and university educators and administrators work to create space where critical media literacy can be part of the process of becoming a teacher and will get worked into curriculum development and lesson planning. This manifesto and its journey are intended to be the first steps. Let us work together on what's next.

8   Conclusion

Season 4 of HBO's 5-season *The Wire*, which chronicles the Baltimore, Maryland drug trade, focused on the public schools, highlighting four young men at a pivotal moment in their lives: They were primed for roles in the drug business, or could choose a less glamorous, but (potentially) more stable school-focused life. On the first day back after summer vacation, a silent montage of empty hallways, classrooms, and the cafeteria introduces the audience to the school setting. The camera finally rests on Assistant Principal Marcia Donnelly (Susan Duvall), holding a walkie-talkie and looking at her watch. The silence is broken with the opening bell when the hallways flood with majority black and brown youth, wearing their uniform of khakis and different colored polo shirts to indicate grade. Donnelly hollers above the din of school kids, reminding each grade where to go to get to homeroom. On his first day of 8th grade, Namond Brice (Julitto McCullum), son of Roland "Weebay" Brice, a loyal soldier to drug kingpin Avon Barksdale, defies the school dress code by wearing oversized diamond earrings, an oversized gold chain, and a football jersey over his regulation maroon polo. Namond mocks a school security guard, who swats him on the back of his head. Namond laughs and says, "Yo, I love the first day of school, son. Everyone's all friendly and shit." Donnelly reprimands Namond for his dress code violation and he takes off the jersey and earrings and tucks the necklace into his polo. Both Donnelly and Namond are unfazed by the behavioral infraction and Namond continues his conversation with Mike (Tristan Mack Wilds), Dukie (Jermaine Crawford), and Randy (Maestro Harrell) as they make their way to homeroom. Over the course of the season, the intertwined lives of these young men is played out with moments of great joy and heart-wrenching agony.

What can be learned from the show and this scene in particular?

The five-season series originally ran from 2002–2009, on HBO, a pay-cable channel. At that time, the majority of us were watching TV *on* television and the episodes were only available on HBO. As of this writing, the series in its entirety can be streamed with an HBO or Amazon Prime account. While the show was critically acclaimed for its realistic and complex portrayal of the Baltimore, Maryland drug trade (Shelley, 2005), it did not always get high ratings (Guthrie, 2004). Those low ratings may have been because of the intricate story lines that developed over the five seasons; they may have been because of the show's predominantly black and brown cast, many of whom were relatively unknown actors at the time; they may have been because of the high cost of an HBO subscription, on top of the standard cable package. While the cast was predominantly black and brown and spoke in the vernacular and colloquialisms of the street, the creators, producers, and lead writers were white men and women. The two creators, David Simon and Ed Burns, came by their storylines honestly via immersive history: Simon was a journalist, covering the drug trade, for many years in Baltimore; Burns was a Baltimore police officer-turned-public school teacher. According to HBO's promotional materials for the show, one of the key reasons to watch is to "Learn a second language. 'Burners,' 'G-packs' and 'hand-to-hands' will be second nature (Subtitles are your friend!)" (Armstrong & Silva, n.d., hbo.com). Black and brown vernacular is (once again) co-opted for entertainment. The behind-the-scenes exploration of *The Wire* begs the question: For whom is the telling of the highly sophisticated, detailed study of the Baltimore drug trade? Can a show be 'good' in content and representation while having contradictory production elements?

In exploring the highlighted scene in particular, we see that school is not just its classrooms and hallways and staff. The cacophony of school children is what makes a school alive. Even on the first day, administrators may suffer from exhaustion and cling to seemingly arbitrary rules and regulations – wear the right clothes, use the correct staircases and hallways – to establish order and maintain structure. School definitely interrupts summer and its flexible timing and potential to earn money – but it is a safe and familiar space. Despite being the son of a notorious drug dealer, all but assuring his leadership in the drug trade, dress code and conformity still apply to Namond. In just a few moments, with minimal dialogue, a rich and robust scene is painted: Education *is* the answer. It is now our responsibility to ask better questions.

Note

1   The now-defunct Channel 1 was founded by H. Christopher Whittle who, after its demise, found the for-profit Edison Schools, discussed in Chapter 3. The Discovery Channel is a pay-television channel. Nickelodeon is a pay-television channel owned by Viacom, one of the 'Big 6.' Google is the primary search engine on most web platforms as well as a producer of software and hardware.

References

Achinstein, B., & Ogawa, R. T. (2011). *Change(d) agents: New teachers of color in urban schools*. New York, NY: Teachers College Press.

Adorno, T. (1991). *The culture industry*. London: Routledge.

Alexander, M. (2010). *The new Jim Crow: Mass incarceration in the age of colorblindness*. New York, NY: The New Press.

Alonso, G., Anderson, N. S., Su, C., & Theoharris, J. (2009). *Our schools suck: Students talk back to a segregated nation on the failures of urban education*. New York, NY: NYU Press.

Althusser, L. (1970). *'Lenin and philosophy' and other essays*. New York, NY: Monthly Review Press.

An act concerning media literacy. (2013). Massachusetts bill #S213/H472. Retrieved from https://malegislature.gov/Bills/188/H472/FiscalNote

An act concerning the teaching of media literacy. (2014). New Jersey bill #S1761. Retrieved from https://www.njleg.state.nj.us/2014/Bills/S2000/1761_I1.htm

An act to involve youth in civic engagement. (2014). Massachusetts bill #S2027. Retrieved from https://malegislature.gov/Bills/188/S2027

Anderson, M., & Jiang, J. (2018, May 31). Teens, social media and technology 2018. Pew Research Center. Retrieved June 1, 2018, from https://www.pewinternet.org/2018/05/31/teens-social-media-technology-2018/

Anderson, P., & Summerfield, J. P. (2004). Why is urban education different from suburban and rural education? In S. R. Steinberg & J. L. Kincheloe (Eds.), *19 urban questions: Teaching in the city* (pp. 29–39). New York, NY: Peter Lang.

Anyon, J. (1997). *Ghetto schooling: The political economy of urban educational reform*. New York, NY: Teachers College Press.

Apple, M. W. (2008). Is deliberative democracy enough in teacher education? In M. Cochran-Smith, S. Feiman-Nemser, D. J. McIntyre, & K. Demers (Eds.), *Handbook of research on teacher education: Enduring questions in changing contexts* (3rd ed., pp. 105–110). New York, NY: Routledge and Taylor & Francis Group.

Armstrong, O., & Silva, R. (n.d.). *Stop stalling and watch The Wire*. HBO. Retrieved June 17, 2019, from https://www.hbo.com/the-wire/stop-stalling-and-watch-the-wire

Arther, L. (2005). Popular culture: Views of parents and educators. In J. Marsh (Ed.), *Popular culture, new media, and digital literacy in early childhood education* (pp. 165–182). London: Routledge.

Aufderheide, P. (1993). *Media literacy – A report of the National Leadership Conference on media literacy*. Queenstown, MD. The Aspen Institute.

Aviv, R. (2018, October 1). Georgia's separate and unequal special education system. *New Yorker*, pp. 34–43.

Back to school statistics. (n.d.). National Council for Education Statistics. Retrieved June 1, 2018, from https://nces.ed.gov

Baker, F. (2012). *Media literacy in the K-12 classroom*. Eugene, OR: International Society for Technology in Education.

Bazalgette, C. (1992). Key aspects of media education. In M. Alvarado & O. Boyd-Barrett (Eds.), *Media education: An introduction* (pp. 199–219). London: The Open University Press.

Benner, K., & Green, E. L. (2019, June 12). FBI is said to be investigating college admissions practices at T.M. Landry. *New York Times*. Retrieved June 17, 2019, from https://www.nytimes.com/2019/06/02/us/politics/tm-landry-fbi-college-admissions.html

Berdick, C. (2018, January 22). To ban or not to ban: Teachers grapple with forcing students to disconnect from technology. *The Washington Post*. Retrieved January 22, 2018, from https://www.washingtonpost.com/news/grade-point/wp/2018/01/22/to-ban-or-not-to-ban-teachers-cope-with-students-driven-to-distraction-by-technology/

Bikham, D. S., & Slaby, R. G. (2012). Effects of a media literacy program in the U.S. on children's critical evaluation of unhealthy media messages about violence, smoking, and food. *Journal of Children and Media, 6*(2), 255–271.

Blanchard, O. (2013, September 23). I quit Teach for America. *The Atlantic*. Retrieved October 5, 2018, from https://www.theatlantic.com/education/archive/2013/09/i-quit-teach-for-america/279724/

Bleakley, A., Vaala, S., Jordan, A. B., & Romer, D. (2014). The Annenberg media environment survey: Media access and use in U.S. homes with children and adolescents. In A. B. Jordan & D. Romer (Eds.), *Media and the well-being of children and adolescents* (pp. 1–19). New York, NY: Oxford University Press.

Bowles, N. (2018a, October 26). A dark consensus about screens and kids begins to emerge in Silicon Valley. *The New York Times*. Retrieved October 26, 2018, from https://www.nytimes.com/2018/10/26/style/phones-children-silicon-valley.html

Bowles, N. (2018b, October 26). The digital gap between rich kids and poor kids is not what we expected. *The New York Times*. Retrieved October 26, 2018, from https://www.nytimes.com/2018/10/26/style/digital-divide-screens-schools.html

boyd, d. (2009). *Social media is here to stay ... now what?* Redmond, WA: Microsoft Tech Fest. Retrieved June 20, 2011, from danah.org

boyd, d. (2010, October 23). *Living life in public: Why American teens choose publicity over privacy*. Gothenberg: Association of Internet Researchers. Retrieved June 20, 2011, from danah.org

boyd, d. (2014). *It's complicated: The social lives of networked teens*. New Haven, CT: Yale University Press.

REFERENCES

Brimley, P. (2003). *The worm in the apple: How the teacher unions are destroying American education.* New York, NY: Perennial.

Brown, E., Strauss, V., & Stein, P. (2018, March 10). It was hailed as the national model for school reform. Then the scandals hit. *The Washington Post.* Retrieved March 10, 2018, from https://www.washingtonpost.com/local/education/dc-school-scandals-tell-me-that-its-not-great-and-that-youre-dealing-with-it/2018/03/10/b73d9cf0-1d9e-11e8-b2d9-08e748f892c0_story.html

Brown, J. (1998). Media literacy perspectives. *Journal of Communication, 48*(1), 44–57. https://doi.org.10.1111/j.1460-2466.1998.tb02746.x

Brown, J. D., El-Toukhy, S., & Ortiz, R. (2014). Growing up sexually in a digital world: The risks and benefits of youths' sexual media use. In A. B. Jordan & D. Romer (Eds.), *Media and the well-being of children and adolescents* (pp. 90–108). New York, NY: Oxford University Press.

Buckingham, D. (1990). Media education: From pedagogy to practice. In D. Buckingham (Ed.), *Watching media learning: Making sense of media education* (pp. 3–15). London: The Falmer Press.

Buckingham, D. (1991) Teaching about the media. In D. Lusted (Ed.), *The media studies book: A guide for teachers* (pp. 12–35). London: Routledge.

Buckingham, D. (1993a). *Children talking television: The making of television literacy.* London: The Falmer Press.

Buckingham, D. (1993b). Introduction: Young people and the media. In D. Buckingham (Ed.), *Reading audiences: Young people and the media* (pp. 1–23). Manchester: Manchester University Press.

Buckingham, D. (1998a). Introduction: Fantasies of empowerment? Radical pedagogy and popular culture. In D. Buckingham (Ed.), *Teaching popular culture: Beyond radical pedagogy* (pp. 1–17). London: Routledge.

Buckingham, D. (1998b). Media education in the UK: Moving beyond protectionism. *Journal of Communication, 48*(1), 33–43. https://doi.org.10.1111/j.1460-2466.1998.tb02735.x

Buckingham, D. (2000a). *After the death of childhood: Growing up in the age of electronic media.* Cambridge: Polity Press.

Buckingham, D. (2000b). *The making of citizens: Young people, news and politics.* London: Routledge.

Buckingham, D. (2003). *Media education: Literacy, learning and contemporary culture.* London: Polity Press.

Buckingham, D. (2007). *Beyond technology: Children's learning in the age of digital culture.* London: Polity Press.

Buckingham, D. (2008) Introducing identity. In D. Buckingham (Ed.), *Youth, identity and digital media* (pp. 1–24). Cambridge, MA: MIT Press.

Buckingham, D. (2011). *The material child: Growing up in consumer culture*. Cambridge: Polity Press.

Buckingham, D., Fraser, P., & Mayman, N. (1990). Stepping into the void: Beginning classroom research in media education. In D. Buckingham (Ed.), *Watching media learning* (pp. 19–59). London: The Falmer Press.

Buckingham, D., Grahame, J., & Sefton-Green, J. (1995). *Making media: Practical production in media education*. London: English & Media Centre.

Buckingham, D., & Sefton-Green, J. (1994). *Cultural studies goes to school: Reading and teaching popular culture*. London: Taylor and Francis.

Building a brighter future for millions of kids. (n.d.). *Verizon*. Retrieved October 15, 2018, from https://www.verizon.com/about/responsibility/verizon-innovative-learning/

Burch, A. D. S., & Mazzei, P. (2018, February 14). Death toll is at 17 and could rise in Florida shooting. *The New York Times*. Retrieved February 14, 2018, from https://www.nytimes.com/2018/02/14/us/parkland-school-shooting.html

Burris, C., & Ravitch, D. (2018, November 4). Why it matters who governs America's public schools. *The Washington Post*. Retrieved November 4, 2018, from https://www.washingtonpost.com/education/2018/11/04/why-it-matters-who-governs-americas-public-schools/

Butler, A. (2010). *Media education goes to school: Young people make meaning of media and urban education*. New York, NY: Peter Lang.

Butler, A. (2015). Thinking like a filmmaker: Notes on visual literacy learning and civic engagement. *Youth Media Reporter*. from https://www.youthmediareporter.org/2015/04/08/thinking-like-a-filmmaker-notes-on-visual-literacy-learning-and-civic-engagement/

Butler, A. (2016). Policy, participation and practice: Assessing media literacy in the digital age. In J. Frechette & R. Williams (Eds.), *Media education for a digital generation* (pp. 119–131). New York, NY: Routledge.

Butler, A., Fuentes-Bautista, M., & Scharrer, E. (2018). Building media literacy in higher education: Department approaches, undergraduate certificate, and engaged scholarship. In J. Cubbage (Ed.), *Media literacy in higher education environments* (pp. 153–171). Hershey, PA: IGI Global.

Butler, A., & Ladd, A. (2016). Teacher training, lesson plan development, and classroom integration: Notes on the process of building a media literacy curriculum. *Media Education Research Journal, 6*(2), 14–29.

Calfas, J. (2018, February 18). The teens who survived the Florida school shooting are organizing a national march to demand gun control. *Time*. Retrieved March 1, 2018, from https://time.com/5164939/march-for-our-lives-florida-shooting/

California State legislature. (2013, August 6). *Cardenas introduces legislation to encourage computer education*. Retrieved from https://cardenas.house.gov/media-center/press-releases/c-rdenas-introduces-legislation-to-encourage-computer-education

REFERENCES

Capo Crucet, J. (2018, April 28). Did I choose the wrong college? *The New York Times*. Retrieved April 28, 2018, from https://www.nytimes.com/2018/04/28/opinion/sunday/college-debt-choices.html

Carlson, A., & Patel, J. K. (2018, March 22). March for our lives: Maps of the more than 800 protests around the world. *The New York Times*. Retrieved March 22, 2018, from https://www.nytimes.com/interactive/2018/03/22/us/politics/march-for-lives-demonstrations.html

Cassada, R. (2013, April 7). Teen texting – The real issue. *Psychology Today*. Retrieved October 15, 2018, from https://www.psychologytoday.com/us/blog/teen-angst/201304/teen-sexting-the-real-issue

Clotfelter, C. T., Ladd, H. F., & Vigdor, J. L. (2007, January). *How and why do teacher credentials matter for student achievement?* Cambridge, MA: National Bureau of Economic Research. Retrieved October 15, 2018, from https://www.nber.org/papers/w12828

Collier, A. (2014). Perspectives on parenting in a digital age. In A. B. Jordan & D. Romer (Eds.), *Media and the well-being of children and adolescents* (pp. 247–265). New York, NY: Oxford University Press.

Cornbleth, C. (2014). *Understanding teacher education in contentious times: Political cross-currents and conflicting interests*. New York, NY: Routledge.

Christ, W. G. (2004). Assessment, media literacy standards, and higher education. *American Behavioral Scientist, 48*(1), 92–96.

Chromebook sales to families help raise funds for PTAs. (n.d.). Retrieved November 15, 2018, from https://edu.google.com/products/chromebooks/?modal_active=none

Cookson, P. W., Darling-Hammond, L., Rothman, R., & Shields, P. M. (2018, October). *The tapestry of American public education: How can we create a system of schools worth choosing for all?* Palo Alto, CA: The Learning Policy Institute.

Darling-Hammond, L. (1999/2008). The case for university-based teacher education. In M. Cochran-Smith, S. Feiman-Nemser, D. J. McIntyre, & K. Demers (Eds.), *Handbook of research on teacher education: Enduring questions in changing contexts* (3rd ed., pp. 333–346). New York, NY: Routledge and Taylor & Francis Group.

Darling-Hammond, L. (2000). Teacher quality and student achievement: A review of state policy evidence. *Education Policy Analysis Archives, 8*(1), 1–44.

Darling-Hammond, L. (2006). *Powerful teacher education: Lessons from exemplary programs*. San Francisco, CA: Jossey-Bass.

Darling-Hammond, L. (2010). *The flat world of education: How America's commitment to equity will determine our future*. New York, NY: Teachers College Press.

Darling-Hammond, L. (2011). Developing powerful teaching and learning: Grow your own teachers within the national educational reform context. In E. A. Skinner, M. T. Garretón, & B. A. Schultz (Eds.), *Grow your own teachers: Grassroots change for teacher education* (pp. 163–177). New York, NY: Teachers College Press.

106   REFERENCES

Darling-Hammond, L., Banks, J., Zumwalt, K., Gomez, L., Gamoran-Sherin, M., Griesdorn, J., & Finn, L. E. (2005a). Educational goals and purposes: Developing a curricular vision for teaching. In L. Darling-Hammond & J. Bransford (Eds.), *Preparing teachers for a changing world: What teachers should learn and do* (pp. 169–200). San Francisco, CA: Jossey-Bass.

Darling-Hammond, L., Holtzman, D. J., Gatlin, S. J., & Vasquez-Heilig, J. (2005b). Does teacher preparation matter? Evidence about teacher certification, teach for America, and teacher effectiveness. *Educational Policy Analysis Archives, 13*(42), 1–48.

Darling-Hammond, L., & Rothman, R. (2015). *Teaching in the flat world: Learning from high performing system.* New York, NY: Teachers College Press.

Delpit, L. (2002). No kinda sense. In L. Delpit (Ed.), *The skin that we speak: Thoughts on language and culture in the classroom* (pp. 31–48). New York, NY: The New Press.

DeRousseau, R. (2018, August 2). Apple isn't the first to hit $1 trillion value. Here are five companies that did it earlier. *Yahoo! Finance.* Retrieved October 1, 2018, from https://finance.yahoo.com/news/apple-isn-apos-t-first-162722381.html

DiMartino, C., & Butler-Jessen, S. (2018). *Selling school: The marketing of public education.* New York, NY: Teachers College Press.

Domaille, K., & Buckingham, D. (2001, November). *Youth media education survey 2001,* from http://www.unesco.org/new/fileadmin/MULTIMEDIA/HQ/CI/CI/pdf/youth_media_education.pdf

Douclef, M., & Aubrey, A. (2018, February 12). Smartphone detox: How to power down in a wired world. *National Public Radio.* Retrieved February 14, 2018, from https://www.npr.org/sections/health-shots/2018/02/12/584389201/smartphone-detox-how-to-power-down-in-a-wired-world

Douglass, F. (1845/1995). *Narrative of the life of Frederick Douglass.* Mineola, NY: Dover Publications.

Egan, T. (2018, September 14). The secret to cracking Trump's base. *The New York Times.* Retrieved September 14, 2018, from https://www.nytimes.com/2018/09/14/opinion/trump-base-polls.html

Fairvote (n.d.). *What effects voter turnout rates?* FairVote. Retrieved September 15, 2018, from https://www.fairvote.org/what_affects_voter_turnout_rates

Fast Facts (n.d.). *Council for American Private Education.* Retrieved September 15, 2018, from https://www.capenet.org

Fingar, K., & Jolls, T. (2013). Evaluation of a school-based violence prevention media literacy curriculum. *Injury Prevention, 20,* 183–190. https://dx.doi.org/10.1136/injuryprev-2013-040815

Finn Jr., C. E. (1999). Forward. In M. Kanstooroom & C. E. Finn Jr. (Eds.), *Better teachers, better schools* (pp. vi–vii). Washington, DC: The Thomas B. Fordham Foundation.

FiveThirtyEight. (2018). *How popular/unpopular is President Trump?* Retrieved September 15, 2018, from https://projects.fivethirtyeight.com/trump-approval-ratings/

REFERENCES

Flanagin, A. J., & Metzger, M. J. (2010). *Kids and credibility: An empirical examination of youth, digital media use, and information credibility.* Cambridge, MA: MIT Press.

Frechette, J., & Williams, R. (Eds.), *Media education for a digital generation.* New York, NY: Routledge.

Freire, P. (1970). *Pedagogy of the oppressed.* New York, NY: Continuum International Publishing Group, Inc.

From the classroom to the living room. (n.d.). *Google.* Retrieved October 1, 2018, from https://edu.google.com/products/chromebooks/?modal_active=none

Fuller-Ossoli, M. (1855/2017). *Woman in the nineteenth century and kindred papers relating to the sphere, condition, and duties of woman.* London: Forgotten Books.

Garfield, L. (2018, May 12). Mark Zuckerberg once made a $100 million investment in a major U.S. city to help fix its schools – Now the mayor says the effort 'parachuted' in and failed. *Business Insider.* Retrieved October 1, 2018, from https://www.businessinsider.com/mark-zuckerberg-schools-education-newark-mayor-ras-baraka-cory-booker-2018-5

Gerald, C. (2018, December 8). TM Landry and the tragedy of viral success stories. *The New York Times.* Retrieved December 8, 2018, from https://www.nytimes.com/2018/12/08/opinion/sunday/tm-landry-louisiana-school-abuse.html

Gillen, J. (2014). *Educating for insurgency: The roles of young people in schools of poverty.* Oakland, CA: AK Press.

Giroux, H. (2007). Drowning democracy: The media, neoliberalism and the politics of Hurricane Katrina. In D. Macedo & S. Steinberg (Eds.), *Media literacy: A reader* (pp. 229–241). New York, NY: Peter Lang.

Giroux, H. (2009). *Youth in a suspect society: Democracy or disposability?* New York, NY: Palgrave MacMillan.

Goodman, M. (2015). *Future crimes: Everything is connected, everyone is vulnerable, and what we can do about it.* New York, NY: Doubleday.

Goodman, S. (2003). *Teaching youth media: A critical guide to literacy, video production, and social change.* New York, NY: Teachers College Press.

Grahame, J. (1991). The production process. In D. Lusted (Ed.), *The media studies book: A guide for teachers* (pp. 146–170). London: Routledge.

Green, E. (2014). *Building a better teacher: How teaching works (and how to teach it to everyone).* New York, NY: WW Norton & Company.

Green, E., & Benner, K. (2018, November 30). Louisiana school made headlines for sending black kids to elite colleges. Here's the reality. *The New York Times.* Retrieved November 30, 2018, from https://www.nytimes.com/2018/11/30/us/tm-landry-college-prep-black-students.html

Guthrie, M. (2004, December 15). 'The Wire' fears HBO may snip it. *New York Daily News.* Retrieved June 17, 2019, from http://www.nydailynews.com/archives/entertainment/wire-fears-hbo-snip-article-1.608149

Hall, S., & Jefferson, T. (Eds.). (1976). *Resistance through rituals*. London: Routledge.

Hall, S., & Whannell, P. (1965). *The popular arts*. New York, NY: Pantheon Books.

Halloran, J. D., & Jones, M. (1986/1992). The inoculation approach. In M. Alvarado & O. Boyd-Barrett (Eds.), *Media education: An introduction* (pp. 10–13). London: The Open University.

Hansen, D. T. (2008). Values and purpose in teacher education. In M. Cochran-Smith, S. Feiman-Nemser, D. J. McIntyre, & K. Demers (Eds.), *Handbook of research on teacher education: Enduring questions in changing contexts* (3rd ed., pp. 10–26). New York, NY: Routledge and Taylor & Francis Group.

Harvey, D. (2005). *A brief history of neoliberalism*. Oxford: Oxford University Press.

Hayes-Jacobs, H. (2014). *Mastering media literacy*. Bloomington, IN: Solution Tree Press.

Hebdige, D. (1979). *Subcultures: The meaning of style*. London: Routledge.

Hobbs, R. (1998). The seven great debates in the media literacy movement. *Journal of Communication, 48*(1), 16–32. https://doi.org.10.1111/j.1460-2466.1998.tb02734

Hobbs, R. (2011a). *Digital and media literacy: Connecting culture and classroom*. Thousand Oaks, CA: Corwin.

Hobbs, R. (2011b). The state of media literacy: A response to Potter. *Journal of Broadcasting and Electronic Media, 55*(3), 419–430. https://doi.org./10.1080/08838151.2011.597594

Hoechsmann, M., & Poyntz, S. R. (2012). *Media literacies: A critical introduction*. Malden, MA: John Wiley & Sons.

Hoggart, R. (1959). *The uses of literacy*. London: Chatto & Windus.

hooks, b. (1994). *Teaching to transgress: Education as the practice of freedom*. New York, NY: Routledge.

hooks, b. (2003). *Teaching community: A pedagogy of hope*. New York, NY: Routledge.

hooks, b. (2010). *Teaching critical thinking: Practical wisdom*. New York, NY: Routledge.

Horkheimer, M., & Adorno, T. (1947/2002). *Dialectic of enlightenment: Philosophical fragments*. Stanford, CA: Stanford University Press.

Howell, W. G. (2015). Results of President Obama's race to the top. *Education Next, 15*(4), Fall. from https://www.educationnext.org/results-president-obama-race-to-the-top-reform/

Ingalls-Wilder, L. (1943). *These happy golden years*. New York, NY: HarperCollins.

Ingles, P. (2001, July 14). Corporate media literacy. *On the Media*. New York: WNYC Studios. Retrieved October 1, 2018, from https://www.wnycstudios.org/story/132071-corporate-media-literacy

iPad in the classroom. (n.d.) Retrieved from https://www.apple.com/ca/education/

Jackson, A. (2016, February 21). Teacher at New York City high school has a serious beef with Teach for America – here's why. *Business Insider*. Retrieved from https://www.businessinsider.sg/gary-rubinstein-discusses-whats-wrong-with-teach-for-america-2016-2/

REFERENCES

Jeffries, D. (2013, March 11). Is technology and the internet reducing pupils' attention spans? *The Guardian.* Retrieved November 1, 2018, from https://www.theguardian.com/teacher-network/teacher-blog/2013/mar/11/technology-internet-pupil-attention-teaching

Jenkins, H., Purushotma, R., Clinton, K., Weigel, M., & Robison, A. (2006). *Confronting the challenges of participatory culture: Media education for the 21st century.* Chicago, IL: The MacArthur Foundation, from https://www.macfound.org/media/article_pdfs/JENKINS_WHITE_PAPER.PDF

Jeong, S. H., Cho, H., & Hwang, Y. (2012). Media literacy interventions: A meta-analytic review. *Journal of Communication, 62*(3), 454–472. https://doi.org.10.1111/j.1460-2466.2012.01643.x

Jhally, S., & Earp, J. (2003). *Empowering literacy: Media education as a democratic imperative.* A report commissioned by the Ford Foundation. Retrieved from mdlab2014.files.wordpress.com

Johnson, S., Campbell, N., & Sargrad, S. (2018, February 12). Trump and DeVos continue to undermine public education with their proposed fiscal year 2019 budget. *Center for American Progress.* Retrieved October 1, 2018, from https://www.americanprogress.org/issues/education-k-12/news/2018/02/12/446423/trump-devos-continue-undermine-public-education-proposed-fiscal-year-2019-budget/

Jolls, T. (2011, March 10). *Voices of media literacy: International pioneers speak.* Center for Media Literacy. Retrieved October 1, 2018, from http://www.medialit.org/reading-room/voices-media-literacy-international-pioneers-speak-renee-hobbs-interview-transcript

Jones, M. (2018, February 7). What teenagers are learning from online porn. *The New York Times.* Retrieved February 7, 2018, from https://www.nytimes.com/2018/02/07/magazine/teenagers-learning-online-porn-literacy-sex-education.html

Kaiser Family Foundation. (2010, January 20). *Daily media use among children and teens up dramatically from five years ago.* Retrieved October 1, 2018, from https://www.kff.org/disparities-policy/press-release/daily-media-use-among-children-and-teens-up-dramatically-from-five-years-ago/

Keiser, D. L. (2005). Learners not widgets: Teacher education for social justice during transformational times. In N. M. Michelli & D. L. Keiser (Eds.), *Teacher education for democracy and social justice* (pp. 31–55). New York, NY: Routledge.

Kellner, D., & Share, J. (2007). Critical media literacy, democracy, and the reconstruction of education. In D. Macedo & S. Steinberg (Eds.), *Media literacy: A reader* (pp. 3–23). New York, NY: Peter Lang.

Klass, P. (2018, March 12). Teenagers are sexting – Now what? *The New York Times.* Retrieved March 12, 2018, from https://www.nytimes.com/2018/03/12/well/family/teens-are-sexting-now-what.html

110 REFERENCES

Klein, J., Rhee, M., with Gorman, P. C., Huberman, R., Johson, C. R., Alonso, A. R., ... Sheffield, L. V. (2010, October 10). How to fix our schools: A manifesto by Joel Klein, Michelle Rhee, and other education leaders. *The Washington Post*. Retrieved November 4, 2018, from http://www.washingtonpost.com/wp-dyn/content/article/2010/10/07/AR2010100705078.html?noredirect=on

Klein, N. (2007). *The shock doctrine: The rise of disaster capitalism*. New York, NY: Metropoiitan Books.

Kohl, H. (2002). Topsy-turvies: Teacher talk and student talk. In L. Delpit (Ed.), *The skin that we speak: Thoughts on language and culture in the classroom* (pp. 145–161). New York, NY: The New Press.

Kozol, J. (1991). *Savage inequalities: Children in America's schools*. New York, NY: Crown Publishers.

Kubey, R. (1998). Obstacles to the development of media education in the United States. *Journal of Communication, 48*(1), 58–69. https://doi.org.10.1111/j.1460-2466.1998.tb02737.x

Labaree, D. F. (2008). An uneasy relationship: The history of teacher education in the university. In M. Cochran-Smith, S. Feiman-Nemser, D. J. McIntyre, & K. Demers (Eds.), *Handbook of research on teacher education: Enduring questions in changing contexts* (3rd ed., pp. 290–306). New York, NY: Routledge and Taylor & Francis Group.

Leavis, F. R., & Thompson, D. (1933). *Culture and environment: The training of critical awareness*. London: Chatto and Windus.

Leonhardt, D., & Chinoy, S. (2019, May 23). The college dropout crisis. *New York Times*. Retrieved May 23, 2019, from https://www.nytimes.com/interactive/2019/05/23/opinion/sunday/college-graduation-rates-ranking.html

Lewis, J., & Jhally, S. (1998). The struggle over media literacy. *Journal of Communication 48*(1), 109–120. https://doi.org.10.1111/j.1460-2466.1998.tb02741.x

Linklater, R. (Director). (2003). *School of rock*. Paramount Pictures.

Litman-Navarro, K. (2019, June 12). We read 150 privacy policies. They were an incomprehensible disaster. *New York Times*. Retrieved June 12, 2019, from https://www.nytimes.com/interactive/2019/06/12/opinion/facebook-google-privacy-policies.html

Livingstone, S. (2004). Media literacy and the challenges of new information and communication technologies. *Communication Review, 7*(1), 3–14. doi:10.1080/10714420490280152

Livingstone, S. (2014). Risk and harm on the internet. In A. B. Jordan & D. Romer (Eds.), *Media and the well-being of children and adolescents* (pp. 129–146). New York, NY: Oxford University Press.

Livingstone, S. (2018, July 27). Media literacy – Everyone's favorite solution to the problems of regulation. *Parenting for a Digital Future*. Retrieved from

REFERENCES

https://blogs.lse.ac.uk/mediapolicyproject/2018/05/08/media-literacy-everyones-favourite-solution-to-the-problems-of-regulation/

Locke, J. (1693/2011). Some thoughts concerning education. In S. M. Cahn (Ed.), *Classic and contemporary readings in the philosophy of education* (2nd ed., pp. 105–121). New York, NY: Oxford University Press.

Long, D., & Riegle, R. (2002). *Teacher education: The key to effective school reform.* Westport, CT: Bergin & Garvey.

Lucas, C. J. (1997). *Teacher education in America: Reform agenda for the twenty-first century.* New York, NY: St. Martin's Press.

Lueck, A. (2018, October 23). How high schools shaped American cities. *The Atlantic.* Retrieved October 23, 2018, from https://www.theatlantic.com/technology/archive/2018/10/how-high-schools-shaped-american-cities/573616/

Macedo, D., & Steinberg, S. (Eds.). (2007). *Media literacy: A reader.* New York, NY: Peter Lang.

Massachusetts Department of Elementary and Secondary Education. (2018). *Massachusetts History and Social Science Curriculum Framework.* Retrieved October 1, 2018, from http://www.doe.mass.edu/frameworks/hss/2018-12.pdf

Masterman, L. (1980). *Teaching about television.* London: The MacMillan Press.

Masterman, L. (1985). *Teaching the media.* London: Routledge.

Mazzarella, S. R. (2008). Introduction: It's a girlwide web. In S. R. Mazzarella (Ed.), *Girl wide web: Girls, the internet and negotiations of identity* (pp. 1–12). New York, NY: Peter Lang.

McRobbie, A. (1976). Girls and subcultures: An exploration. In S. Hall & T. Jefferson (Eds.), *Resistance through rituals* (pp. 209–222). London: Routledge.

Media literacy as an elective in public schools. (2011). New Mexico bill #233. Retrieved from https://nmlegis.gov/Legislation/Legislation?Chamber=H&LegType=B&-LegNo=233&year=11

Media literacy week. (n.d.). *NAMLE.* Retrieved November 1, 2018, from https://namle.net/publications/media-literacy-week-november-2nd-6th-2015/

Mehta, J. (2013, April 12). Teachers: Will we ever learn? *The New York Times.* Retrieved November 15, 2018, from https://www.nytimes.com/2013/04/13/opinion/teachers-will-we-ever-learn.html

Mehta, J. (2016). The courage to achieve our ambitions: Five pathways for the future. In J. Mehta, R. B. Schwartz, & F. M. Hess (Eds.), *The futures of school reform* (pp. 177–210). Cambridge, MA: Harvard Education Press.

Mehta, J., Schwartz, R. B., & Hess, F. M. (2016). Introduction: The futures of school reform. In J. Mehta, R. B. Schwartz, & F. M. Hess (Eds.), *The futures of school reform* (pp. 1–11). Cambridge, MA: Harvard Education Press.

MetLife Inc. (2011, May). *The MetLife survey of the American teacher: Preparing students for college and careers.* Retrieved July 8, 2018, from https://files.eric.ed.gov/fulltext/ED519278.pdf

MetLife Inc. (2013, February). *The MetLife survey of the American teacher: Challenges for school leadership*. Retrieved July 8, 2018, from https://www.metlife.com/content/dam/microsites/about/corporate-profile/MetLife-Teacher-Survey-2012.pdf

Michaelmore, K., & Dynarski, S. (2017, April 20). Income differences in education: The gap within the gap. *Education Policy*. Retrieved June 15, 2018, from https://econofact.org/income-differences-in-education-the-gap-within-the-gap

Microsoft schools program. (n.d.). *Microsoft*. Retrieved October 1, 2018, from https://www.microsoft.com/en-us/education/school-leaders/showcase-schools

MIT Education Data and Science Lab. (n.d.). *Voter turnout*. Retrieved November 1, 2018, from https://electionlab.mit.edu/research/voter-turnout

Montgomery, K. C. (2007). *Generation digital: Politics, commerce and childhood in the age of the internet*. Cambridge, MA: MIT Press.

Moore, B. (1991). Media education. In D. Lusted (Ed.), *The media studies book: A guide for teachers* (pp. 171–190). London: Routledge.

Murrow, E. R. (1958, October 15). *Wires and lights in a box*. Radio Television Digital News Association. Retrieved from https://www.rtdna.org/content/edward_r_murrow_s_1958_wires_lights_in_a_box_speech

NAMLE conference. (n.d.). *NAMLE*. Retrieved November 1, 2018, from https://namleconference.net

National Commission on Excellence in Education. (1983). *A nation at risk: The imperative for educational reform*. Washington, DC: U.S. Department of Education. Retrieved August 20, 2018, from edreform.com/wp-content/uploads/2013/02/A_Nation_At_Risk_1983_PDF

National Communication Association. (1998). *K-12 speaking, listening and media literacy standards and competency statements*. Retrieved October 10, 2018, from natcom/org/sites/default/files/pages/Public_Statements_K-12Standards.pdf

Nation's students to give American education system yet another chance. (2011, August 17). *The Onion*. Retrieved August 20, 2018, from https://kinja.com/api/profile/getsession?redirect=https%3A%2F%2Flocal.theonion.com%2Fsetsession%3Fr%3Dhttps%253A%252F%252Flocal.theonion.com%252Fnations-students-to-give-american-education-system-yet-1819572881

Nazaryan, A. (2016, August 10). Carmen Farina, New York City's school chief, and the perils of school reform. *Newsweek*. Retrieved September 1, 2018, from https://www.newsweek.com/2016/08/19/charters-schools-nyc-488880.html

Olen, H. (2018, May 16). Betsy DeVos knows little about public education., & she doesn't want to learn. *The Washington Post*. Retrieved May 16, 2018, from https://www.washingtonpost.com/blogs/plum-line/wp/2018/05/16/betsy-devos-knows-little-about-public-education-and-she-doesnt-want-to-learn/

Orenstein, P. (2016). *Girls and sex: Navigating the complicated new landscape*. New York, NY: Harper Collins.

REFERENCES

Otterman, S. (2016, January 14). Joel Klein, ex-New York schools' chancellor, to join health insurance start-up. *The New York Times*. Retrieved November 15, 2018, from https://www.nytimes.com/2016/01/15/nyregion/joel-klein-ex-new-york-schools-chancellor-to-join-health-insurance-start-up.html

Pasquale, F. (2015). *The Black box society: The secret algorithms that control money and information*. Cambridge, MA: Harvard University Press.

Patton, D. (2014, February 21). The myth behind public school failure. *Yes! Magazine*. Retrieved November 15, 2018, from https://www.yesmagazine.org/issues/education-uprising/the-myth-behind-public-school-failure

Perez-Pena, R. (2010, September 22). Facebook founder to donate $100 million to help remake Newark's schools. *The New York Times*. Retrieved November 15, 2018, from https://www.nytimes.com/2010/09/23/education/23newark.html

Phillips, M. (2018, August 2). Apple's $1 trillion milestone reflects rise of powerful megacorporations. *New York Times*. Retrieved August 2, 2018, from https://www.nytimes.com/2018/08/02/business/apple-trillion.html

Phillips, P. (2018). *Giants: The global power elite*. New York, NY: Seven Stories Press.

Postman, N. (1985). *Amusing ourselves to death: Public discourse in the age of show business*. New York, NY: Penguin.

Postman, N. (1994). *The disappearance of childhood*. New York, NY: Knopf.

Potter, J. (2012) *Digital media and learner identity: The new curatorship*. New York, NY: Palgrave MacMillan.

Potter, W. J. (1998). *Media literacy*. Thousand Oaks, CA: Sage Publications.

Potter, W. J. (2010). The state of media literacy. *Journal of Broadcasting and Electronic Media, 54*(4), 675–696. https://doi.org.10.1080/08838151.2011.521462

Priddy, B. (n.d.). The growing problem of smartphone addiction. *Tech Addiction*. Retrieved November 15, 2018, from http://www.techaddiction.ca/smartphone-addiction-problem.html

Project for Excellence in Journalism. (2008). *The state of the news media 2008: An annual report on American journalism*. Pew Internet Research. Retrieved October 1, 2018, from https://assets.pewresearch.org/wp-content/uploads/sites/13/2017/05/24141607/State-of-the-News-Media-Report-2008-FINAL.pdf

Public Broadcasting System. (2007). *Democracy on deadline: Who owns the media?* Retrieved October 1, 2018, from https://www.pbs.org/independentlens/democracyondeadline/mediaownership.html

Public school media literacy classes. (2009). New Mexico bill #342. Retrieved from https://nmlegis.gov/Legislation/Legislation?Chamber=H&LegType=B&LegNo=342&year=09

Ravitch, D. (1974/2000). *The great school wars: A history of the New York City public schools*. Baltimore, MD: Johns Hopkins University Press.

Ravitch, D. (1983). *The troubled crusade: American education 1945–1980*. New York, NY: Basic Books.

Ravitch, D. (2010). *The death and life of the great American school system: How testing and choice are undermining education*. New York, NY: Perseus Books.

Rhee, M., & Oakley, K. (2008). Rigor and relevance in teacher preparation. In M. Cochran-Smith, S. Feiman-Nemser, D. J. McIntyre, & K. Demers (Eds.), *Handbook of research on teacher education: Enduring questions in changing contexts* (3rd ed., pp. 373–378). New York, NY: Routledge and Taylor & Francis Group.

Richmond, E. (2018, February 13). Does Trump's education budget even matter? *Educational Writers Association*. Retrieved March 15, 2018, from https://www.ewa.org/blog-educated-reporter/does-trumps-education-budget-even-matter

Ripley, A. (2008, November 26). Rhee tackles classroom challenges. *Time*. Retrieved November 10, 2010, from http://content.time.com/time/magazine/article/0,9171,1862444,00.html

Robertson, E. (2008). Teacher education in a democratic society: Learning and teaching the practices of democratic participation. In M. Cochran-Smith, S. Feiman-Nemser, D. J. McIntyre, & K. Demers (Eds.), *Handbook of research on teacher education: Enduring questions in changing contexts* (3rd ed., pp. 27–44). New York, NY: Routledge and Taylor & Francis Group.

Rothstein, R. (2012, October 11). Joel Klein's misleading autobiography. *The American Prospect*. Retrieved November 15, 2018, from https://prospect.org/article/joel-kleins-misleading-autobiography

Rothstein, R. (2018, February 12). How to fix our schools. *Economic policy institute*. Retrieved November 15, 2018, from https://www.epi.org/publication/ib286/

Rousseau, J. J. (1962/2011). Emile, or education (W. Boyd, Trans.). In S. M. Cahn (Ed.), *Classic and contemporary readings in the philosophy of education* (2nd ed., pp. 122–152). New York, NY: Oxford University Press.

Rozsa, L., & Zezima, K. (2018, June 4). March for Our Lives plans to barnstorm the country with voting drives this summer. *The Washington Post*. Retrieved June 4, 2018, from https://www.washingtonpost.com/news/post-nation/wp/2018/06/04/march-for-our-lives-plans-to-barnstorm-the-country-with-voting-drives-this-summer/

Rubin, A. M. (Ed.). (1998). *Journal of Communication, 48*(1). Special issue on media literacy.

Sadowski, M. (2016). *Safe is not enough: Better schools for LGBTQ students*. Cambridge, MA: Harvard University Press.

Sales, N. J. (2016). *American girls: Social media and the secret life of teenagers*. New York, NY: Alfred A. Knopf.

Salinas, S., & D'Onfro, J. (2018, November 28). Google employees: We no longer believe the company places values over profits. *CNBC*. Retrieved November 30, 2018, from https://www.cnbc.com/2018/11/27/read-google-employees-open-letter-protesting-project-dragonfly.html

REFERENCES

Saltman, K. (2010). *The gift of education: Public education and venture philanthropy.* New York, NY: Palgrave MacMillan.

Scharrer, E. (2002). Making a case for media literacy in the curriculum: Outcomes and assessments. *Journal of Adolescent and Adult Literacy, 46*(4), 354–358.

Scharrer, E., Olson, C. J., Sekarasih, L., & Cadrette, R. (2016). Encouraging critical thinking through cyberbullying: Media literacy data from 6th graders. In J. Frechette & R. Williams (Eds.), *Media education for a digital generation* (pp. 143–156). New York, NY: Routledge.

Scheff, S. (2017, December 22). Top health concern for parents: Bullying, cyberbullying and internet safety. *The Huffington Post.* Retrieved November 30, 2018, from https://www.huffpost.com/entry/top-health-concern-for-parents-bullying-cyberbullying_b_5a3d7681e4b0df0de8b06522

Schmidt, H. (2012). Media literacy education at the university level. *The Journal of Effective Teaching, 12*(1), 64–77.

Schofield-Clark, L. (2008). The constant contact generation: Exploring teen friendship networks online. In S. R. Mazzarella (Ed.), *Girl wide web: Girls, the internet and negotiations of identity* (pp. 203–221). New York, NY: Peter Lang.

Schofield-Clark, L. (2014, March 12). Banning kids from having smartphones misses the point. *Psychology Today.* Retrieved September 30, 2018, from https://www.psychologytoday.com/us/blog/parenting-in-digital-age/201403/banning-kids-having-smartphones-misses-the-point

Schultz, B. A., Gillette, M. D., & Hill, D. A. (2011). Teaching as political: Theoretical perspectives for understanding the Grow Your Own Movement. In E. A. Skinner, M. T. Garretón, & B. A. Schultz (Eds.), *Grow your own teachers: Grassroots change for teacher education* (pp. 5–21). New York, NY: Teachers College Press.

Shah, A. (2012, January 28). Media in the United States. *Global Issues.* Retrieved September 1, 2018, from http://www.globalissues.org/article/163/media-in-the-united-states

Shelley, J. (2005, August 5). Call the cops. *The Guardian.* Retrieved June 17, 2019, from https://www.theguardian.com/media/2005/aug/06/tvandradio.guide2

Singer, N., & Maheshwari, S. (2018, October 23). Google is teaching children how to act online. Is it the best role model? *The New York Times.* Retrieved October 23, 2018, from https://www.nytimes.com/2018/10/23/business/google-kids-online-safety.html

Skinner, E. A., & Schultz, B. D. (2011). Rethinking teacher preparation. In E. A. Skinner, M. T. Garretón, & B. A. Schultz (Eds.), *Grow your own teachers: Grassroots change for teacher education* (pp. 1–4). New York, NY: Teachers College Press.

Sockett, H. T. (2001). Transforming teacher education. In H. T. Sockett, E. K. DeMulder, P. LePage, & D. R. Wood (Eds.), *Transforming teacher education: Lessons in professional development* (pp. 1–9). Westport, CT: Bergin and Garvey.

Solomon, L. D. (2002). Edison schools and the privatization of K-12 public education: A legal and policy analysis. *Fordham Urban Law Journal, 30*(4), 1281–1340.

Sotomayor, S. (2013). *My beloved world.* New York, NY: Vintage Books.

Stelter, B. (2018, March 20). Google unveils plans to boost news subscriptions and combat fake news. *CNN Business.* Retrieved March 20, 2018, from https://money.cnn.com/2018/03/20/media/google-news-initiative/index.html

Stillman, S. (2016, March 14). The list: When juveniles are found guilty of sexual misconduct, the sex-offender registry can be a life sentence. *New Yorker.* Retrieved October 1, 2018, from https://www.newyorker.com/magazine/2016/03/14/when-kids-are-accused-of-sex-crimes

Stossel, J. (2018, May 9). What haters don't get about Betsy DeVos. *Fox News.* Retrieved May 9, 2018, from https://www.foxnews.com/opinion/john-stossel-what-haters-dont-get-about-betsy-devos

Strauss, S. (2017, December 6). The connection between education, income inequality, and unemployment. *The Huffington Post.* Retrieved October 1, 2018, from https://www.huffpost.com/entry/the-connection-between-ed_b_1066401

Strauss, V. (2014, March 14). Netflix's Reed Hastings has a big idea: Kill elected school boards. *The Washington Post.* Retrieved November 15, 2018, from https://www.washingtonpost.com/news/answer-sheet/wp/2014/03/14/netflixs-reed-hastings-has-a-big-idea-kill-elected-school-boards/?noredirect=on

Teach for America. (n.d.). Retrieved August 20, 2018, from https://www.teachforamerica.org

Terms of service. (n.d.). *SnapChat.* Retrieved October 15, 2018, from https://www.snap.com/en-US/terms/

The Thomas B. Fordham Foundation. (1999). The teachers we need and how to get more of them: A manifesto. In M. Kanstooroom & C. E. Finn Jr. (Eds.), *Better teachers, better schools* (pp. 1–18). Washington, DC: The Thomas B. Fordham Foundation.

The Network for Public Education (NPE) Action. (2018). *Hijacked by billionaires: How the super rich elites buy elections to undermine schools* (An NPE action report). Retrieved November 15, 2018, from https://npeaction.org/wp-content/uploads/2018/09/Hijacked-by-Billionaires.pdf

Toobin, J. (2018, November 19). After Trump. *The New Yorker,* pp. 22–28.

Turkle, S. (2011). *Alone together: Why we expect more from technology and less from each other.* New York, NY: Basic Books.

Tyner, K. (1998). *Literacy in a digital world: Teaching and learning in the age of information.* Mahwah, NJ: Lawrence Erlbaum Associates.

Tyner, K. (2015). Mapping the field of youth media: Results of an environmental scan of youth media organizations in the United States. *Youth Media Reporter.* Retrieved from http://www.youthmediareporter.org/2015/04/08/mapping-the-field-of-youth-media-results-of-an-environmental-scan-of-youth-media-organizations-in-the-united-states/

REFERENCES

Wartella, E., & Lauricella, A. R. (2014). Early learning, academic achievement, and children's digital media. In A. B. Jordan & D. Romer (Eds.), *Media and the well-being of children and adolescents* (pp. 173–186). New York, NY: Oxford University Press.

West, J., & the National Council on Disability. (2000, January). *Back to school on civil rights*. Retrieved October 15, 2018, from https://ncd.gov/rawmedia_repository/7bfb3c01_5c95_4d33_94b7_b80171d0b1bc.pdf

Wilkinson, R., & Pickett, K. (2010). *The spirit level: Why greater equality makes societies stronger*. New York, NY: Bloomsbury Books.

Williams, R. (1958/1983). *Culture and society, 1780–1950*. New York, NY: Columbia University Press.

Williams, R. (1961). *The long revolution*. New York, NY: Columbia University Press.

Wineberg, S., McGraw, S., Breakstone, J., & Ortega, T. (2016). *Evaluating information: The cornerstone of civic online reasoning*. Stanford, CA: Stanford Digital Repository. Retrieved January 22, 2017, from http://purl.stanford.edu/fv75lyt5934

Winn, M. (1977). *The plug-in drug: Television, computers and family life*. New York, NY: Penguin.

Wolf-Harlow, C. (2003, January). Education and correctional populations. Bureau of Justice Statistics Special Report. Retrieved November 15, 2018, from https://www.bjs.gov/content/pub/pdf/ecp.pdf

Wollstonecraft, M. (1792/2011). A vindication of the rights of women. In S. M. Cahn (Ed.), *Classic and contemporary readings in the philosophy of education* (2nd ed., pp. 174–184). New York, NY: Oxford University Press.

Wong, A. (2017, January 20). Delving into one of the questions Betsy DeVos couldn't answer. *The Atlantic*. Retrieved August 15, 2018, from https://www.theatlantic.com/education/archive/2017/01/delving-into-one-of-the-questions-betsy-devos-couldnt-answer/513941/

Wong, A. (2018, August 7). Arne Duncan: 'Everyone says they value education, but their actions don't follow.' *The Atlantic*. Retrieved August 15, 2018, from https://www.theatlantic.com/education/archive/2018/08/arne-duncan-how-schools-work/566987/

Yee, V., & Blinder, A. (2018, March 14). National school walkout: Thousands protest against gun violence. *The New York Times*. Retrieved March 14, 2018, from https://www.nytimes.com/2018/03/14/us/school-walkout.html

Yousman, B. (2016). Who's afraid of critical media literacy? In M. Huff & A. Lee Roth (Eds.), *Censored 2017* (pp. 369–416). New York, NY: Seven Stories Press.

Index

Action Coalition for Media Education (ACME)   73, 91
Alphabet (Google parent company)   2
Amazon   2, 59, 98
Apple   2, 27, 28
Aspen Institute   5

'Big 6'/media conglomeration   2, 11, 16
billionaire education donations   12, 13, 58, 59, 86, 87
Bloomberg, Michael   57, 59
Booker, Corey   59
Brown vs. *Board of Education*   87
Buckingham, David   7–10, 12, 20, 21, 25, 26, 29, 40, 54, 55, 66, 90, 91, 92
Bush, George   87

Carter, Jimmy   87
Channel 1   34, 93, 99
charter schools   12, 13, 37, 40, 45, 46, 53, 56–59, 86, 95
children as consumers   29
Chromebook   27–29
Citizens United   59
Clinton, Bill   26, 87
college readiness   12–14, 19, 57, 67, 68
critical media literacy   4–6, 15, 17–19, 23–26, 29, 54, 70–78, 81–85, 88, 89, 92–97
    and teacher education   4–6, 14, 15, 18, 29, 71–73, 76, 82–97
critical pedagogy   47, 48
critical theory   24
cultural studies   20, 24

DeVos, Betsy   57, 65, 87
    Senate confirmation hearing   65
digital divide   3
Douglass, Frederick   51
Duncan, Arne   57, 65

Edison Schools   34, 69, 90
education
    and voting   53, 58, 79
    of differently-abled students   52, 94

of impoverished students   13–15, 47, 51, 53, 67, 68, 70, 86, 87
of prisoners   52, 53, 68
of queer youth   80, 87, 88, 94
of students of color   32, 46, 47, 51, 53, 67, 87, 94
education schools
    and employment   33, 61
    see also normal schools
Educational Video Center (EVC)   82

Facebook   2, 43, 59, 78, 91
Finn, Chester E.   38
Fisher Family/The Gap   59
Fordham Foundation   37, 38, 44
Freire, Paulo   48, 51, 62
Friedman, Milton   12, 37, 40, 86
Fuller-Ossoli, Margaret   51

Gates Family Foundation/Microsoft   59
Global Action Project (GAP)   82
Global Critical Media Literacy Project (GCMLP)   73, 81, 82, 91
Google   2, 16, 27, 28, 80, 81, 92, 93, 99
Grow Your Own (GYO)   47

Hastings, Reed (Netflix)   58
HBO   16, 97, 98

Instagram   78, 81, 91, 94
iPad   27–29

Jeff Bezos Foundation/Amazon   59

Klein, Joel   27, 57, 65

March for Our Lives   79, 80
Marjory Stoneman Douglass High School   79
Massachusetts Library System (MLS)   75, 76
Massachusetts public schools   31, 74, 75
    Department of Elementary and Secondary Education (DESE)   75
Mass Media Literacy (MML)   73, 91
Masterman, Len   7, 9, 20

INDEX 119

media education   7, 10, 20, 25–27, 82, 83, 87, 92, 94, 95
media literacy   3–11, 14, 15, 18–23, 26, 27, 29, 53, 54, 71–84, 85–99
   celebration   22, 23
   concepts of   7–10, 80
      application of concepts   94–96
   critical media literacy   4–6, 15, 17–19, 23–26, 29, 54, 70–78, 81–85, 88, 89, 92–97
   defensiveness   20, 21
   democratization of   21, 22
   legislation   6, 72
      California   6
      Massachusetts   6
      New Jersey   6
      New Mexico   6
   in Massachusetts   74, 75
   in New York City   74
   media education   7, 10, 20, 25–27, 82, 83, 87, 92, 94, 95
   outside the United States   6, 7
   protectionism   21, 22
   teacher education in   4–6, 14, 15, 18, 29, 71–73, 76, 82–97
Microsoft   2, 16, 27, 59
Murrow, Edward R.   17

A Nation at Risk   12, 55, 56
National Association for Media Literacy Education (NAMLE)   73, 93
National Parent Teacher Association (NPTA)   28
neoliberalism   12, 13, 61
   in education   12–14, 31, 34, 42, 47, 55, 70, 87, 89, 93, 95–97
Netflix (see also Hastings, Reed)   58, 93
Network for Public Education (NPE)   12, 58, 59, 87
New York City public schools   27, 42, 57, 74
Nixon, Richard   86
No Child Left Behind (NCLB)   87
normal schools   33, 61

Obama, Barack   57, 58, 87
The Onion   50, 85
opportunity gap   46, 68

Parent Teacher Association (PTA)   28
Pinterest   78

Project Censored (PC)   73, 81, 82, 91
public schools   5, 11–15, 29, 32, 37, 40–43, 46, 47, 50, 52–54, 58, 59, 61–65, 67–69, 86, 87, 92, 94, 95, 97
   Baltimore, Maryland   48, 98
   Chicago, Illinois   47, 57, 68
   development of   32, 33
   New Orleans, Louisiana   58
   New York, New York   57, 74
   Newark, New Jersey   43
   public school population   11, 12
   reform efforts   53–60
   Washington, D.C.   40, 57

Queer youth   88

Race to the Top   87
Reagan, Ronald   86, 87
Rhee, Michelle   39–41, 57
   Practitioner Teacher Program   39–41

School of Rock   71
See-Hear-Feel-Film (SHFF)   82
SnapChat   78
social media   2, 13–15
   and academic concerns   18, 21
   and popular culture concerns   22, 77
   data mining   28, 81
   use by young people   2, 19, 78–80, 90, 94
Stanford History Education Group (SHEG)   19

Teach for America (TFA)   41–43, 57, 59
Teacher education   4–6, 13–15, 54, 61, 62
   alternative   14, 15, 37–43, 46, 65, 86, 94–96
   media literacy training and   72–76, 81
   traditional   39, 41, 43–46, 49, 94–96
teachers' unions   12, 37, 41–43, 45, 46, 55, 58, 65, 69, 87, 95
teaching
   education history   31, 32
   feminization of   33
   history of   31–35
   teachers' roles   31–35, 60–66, 80, 83
technology in education   23, 26–29
These Happy Golden Years (Laura Ingulls Wilder)   30
T.M. Landry School   13–15
Twitter   91, 93

120   INDEX

Verified Independent News Stories
    (VINS)   81, 82

Walton Family Foundation/Walmart
    58, 59
Whittle, H. Christopher   34, 99
Wilder, Laura Ingalls   30, 85
Winfrey, Oprah   59
The Wire   97–99
"Wires and lights in a box"

young people
    activism (see March for Our Lives)   79,
       80
    living in poverty   3, 13–15
    media use   1–3, 90
    queer youth   88
    student roles/expectations   11, 12, 66,
       67, 77

Zuckerberg, Mark   43, 59